THE BACKYARD TRAEGER COOKBOOK

Your All-in-One Bible to Go from Weekend Griller to Backyard Legend - Packed with Simple and Delicious Recipes for Unforgettable Gatherings. Grill Like a Pro.

TUCKER MCCOY

TABLE OF CONTENTS

CHAPTER 1

INTRODUCTION

MEET THE AUTHOR: TUCKER MCCOY

Tucker McCoy's journey into the grilling world kicked off way before he became a go-to guy for barbecue lovers. Growing up in a family that loved weekend cookouts, he was surrounded by the mouthwatering sounds and smells of grilling from a young age.Those gatherings sparked his passion for whipping up meals that not only filled bellies but also brought family and friends together. The backyard turned into his playground, and the grill became his canvas for culinary creativity.

With over twenty years of hands-on experience under his belt, Tucker has really mastered the art of outdoor cooking. He's especially fond of the **Traeger grill**, which quickly became his favorite because it's so versatile and gives that amazing wood-fired flavor. His journey involved a lot of trial and error, experimenting with different methods, fuel types, and flavor combos to really refine his skills. His expertise comes from a solid understanding of **temperature control** and the unique flavors that different wood pellets, like *hickory* and *mesquite*, bring to the table.

Tucker's approach is a mix of analytical and creative thinking. He's convinced that the key to nailing the perfect grilled dish is all in the details—like knowing the exact temperature to sear a steak for that perfect crust while keeping it juicy inside, or figuring out just how long to smoke a brisket for that tender, melt-in-your-mouth goodness. This attention to detail and his relentless pursuit of excellence have made him a grill master who's eager to share his knowledge with others.

This passion for sharing what he knows led Tucker to write this comprehensive guide. He gets that grilling can feel a bit overwhelming, especially for beginners or anyone looking to up their game. In this book, he breaks everything down into easy-to-follow steps, making the process straightforward. His approachable writing style means even the trickiest techniques are easy to grasp, empowering readers to wow their guests at any gathering.

Tucker's commitment to the craft has caught the eye of the grilling community, with his tips and insights featured in various magazines, reaching a wider audience. He's also been a guest speaker at plenty of BBQ events, where he connects with both newbies and seasoned grillers, offering practical advice and encouragement. His dedication to quality and innovation shines through in this book, giving readers the tools and confidence to become legends in their own backyards.

As you dive into this guide, you'll see that Tucker's love for grilling is infectious. His stories and practical tips go beyond just cooking; they highlight the importance of creating unforgettable experiences and building lasting connections. Whether you're a casual griller looking to sharpen your skills or a pro in search of new ideas, his insights will help you master the art of **Traeger grilling**, turning every meal into a memorable gathering.

WHY THIS BOOK EXISTS

Stepping into your backyard as the sun sets, the smell of wood-fired cooking fills the air, capturing the essence of grilling with a Traeger.

This book is here to help you nail that experience, acting as your go-to guide for becoming a backyard grilling pro, whether you're a weekend warrior or someone who loves throwing unforgettable get-togethers.

Grilling can feel a bit daunting, especially when you're juggling a busy schedule, but with the right tips, it can totally be manageable. This resource breaks down the ins and outs of **Traeger grilling** into simple, actionable steps. You'll go from a casual griller to a confident host, ready to pull off a cookout that'll wow your guests.

Let's talk about something super important: **temperature control**. It's key for getting that perfect sear on a steak or the melt-in-your-mouth texture of a smoked brisket. You'll find detailed instructions on how to manage the heat on a Traeger grill, so you'll know exactly when to crank up the temperature for a quick sear or dial it down for slow cooking. You'll learn to use the built-in temperature controls to make sure every dish hits that sweet spot of doneness.

The type of wood pellets you choose can really change the game, as each one—whether it's *hickory*, *mesquite*, or *apple*—brings its own unique flavor. This guide walks you through the best pairings for different meats and veggies, helping to enhance the natural flavors of your ingredients. You'll develop a keen sense of taste, knowing just which pellets to pick to get that rich, smoky flavor Traeger grills are famous for.

Maintenance is another big topic we cover, because a well-kept grill not only works better but also lasts longer. You'll find practical tips on cleaning and maintaining your Traeger, keeping it in top shape for years to come. Each maintenance step is laid out clearly, making it easy to keep your grill running smoothly with minimal hassle.

Getting to know the unique features of a Traeger grill is crucial for making the most of its capabilities. These grills are super versatile, letting you:

- Grill
- Smoke
- Bake
- Roast
- Braise
- BBQ

This book will help you navigate these features, showing you how to switch between cooking methods effortlessly. You'll gain the confidence to experiment with different techniques, turning every meal into a culinary masterpiece.

By the time you finish this book, you'll have the knowledge and skills to host gatherings that are more than just meals—they'll be memorable experiences. You'll become the go-to person for outdoor cooking, impressing friends and family with your newfound grilling skills. And the best part? You'll do it all without the added stress, fitting it seamlessly into your busy life.

CHAPTER 2

GETTING TO KNOW YOUR TRAEGER GRILL

WHY CHOOSE TRAEGER GRILLS?

When it comes to grilling, Traeger grills have really made a name for themselves, standing out from the crowd. Their advanced technology turns grilling into a precise culinary adventure.

One standout feature is the digital temperature control system, which is a game changer for anyone who struggles to keep the heat steady on traditional grills. With Traeger, you just set your desired temperature, and the grill takes care of the rest, adjusting it within a tight range. This means your food cooks evenly, whether you're searing a steak at high heat or slow-cooking a brisket at lower temps.

Plus, with **WiFIRE® technology**, you can keep an eye on and tweak the grill's temperature right from your smartphone while you whip up other parts of your meal or entertain your guests. This feature gives you the freedom to enjoy your gathering without being glued to the grill. The easy-to-use app lets you set timers, get notifications, and dive into a curated library of recipes made just for Traeger grills.

These tech upgrades not only make grilling more convenient but also cut down on the guesswork that often comes with it. Traditional grills can be a bit unpredictable, with hot spots and fluctuating temperatures leading to uneven cooking. Traeger's precise control systems ensure that every inch of the grill stays at the right temperature, so you can feel confident that your food will come out perfectly every time. This reliability is a big plus for anyone looking to impress family and friends with top-notch meals.

This versatility opens the door to trying out a bunch of cooking techniques and recipes, from smoked ribs to baked desserts, all without needing a bunch of different devices. Basically, they give you the full kitchen experience right in your backyard.

The design and build quality also add to their charm. Made from high-quality materials, Traeger grills are built to handle all kinds of weather and regular use. This sturdy construction means they'll last a long time and perform reliably, which is especially important for those who grill year-round, so you don't have to worry about your gear failing when it matters most.

On top of their solid build, these grills come with user-friendly features that work for both newbies and seasoned grillers. The intuitive controls and clear displays make setup and operation a breeze, even if you're just starting out. The design also includes practical elements that make cleaning and maintenance easy, so you can keep your grill in great shape with minimal hassle.

Traeger grills blend advanced technology, versatility, and durable construction, making them a fantastic choice for anyone looking to up their outdoor cooking game. Whether you're a casual griller or a pro, these grills give you the tools you need to whip up memorable meals with ease.

Setting up a **Traeger grill** is a breeze, even if you're not a tech whiz. The assembly is super user-friendly, so you can quickly put everything together without any hassle and get to grilling in no time. Once it's all set up, the controls are pretty intuitive, making it easy to operate. With just a few button presses, you can pick your cooking temperature, letting the grill handle the heat while you focus on perfecting your recipes instead of wrestling with complicated settings.

Now, let's talk about the heart of the Traeger experience: the **wood pellets**. These little guys are key to giving your food that signature smoky flavor. Traeger has a great variety of pellets, each bringing its own unique taste to the table. For example, *hickory* gives a strong, bold flavor, while *apple* adds a sweeter, milder touch. A handy tip for beginners is to pair stronger flavors like *hickory* or *mesquite* with red meats, while lighter woods like *apple* or *cherry* work wonders with poultry and fish. This flexibility invites you to experiment and find the perfect wood-pellet match for your dishes.

When it comes to maintenance, Traeger makes it easy with a simple-to-clean drip tray and an efficient ash management system that cuts down on the time you spend on upkeep. Just follow these steps to keep your grill in top shape:

- Empty the ash bin every few uses
- Give the drip tray a quick wipe

This way, you can maintain your grill without eating into your precious free time.

What really sets Traeger apart is the awesome community and resources at your fingertips. The Traeger community is a treasure trove of knowledge and inspiration. You'll find everything from detailed online tutorials on the basics to responsive customer service you can reach by phone. Whether you're hunting for new recipes or need some troubleshooting help, there's support available whenever you need it. This network is here to guide you through your grilling journey.

As you get more comfortable with your grill, you'll find yourself connecting with a wider community of fellow outdoor cooking enthusiasts. This sense of belonging not only enhances your experience but also opens up a world of culinary possibilities.

But as you gain confidence, new challenges might pop up. Imagine this: you've nailed the basics, your grill is running like a dream, and your guests can't stop raving about your latest dish. Yet, you can't help but wonder if there are advanced techniques or features that could take your skills to the next level. Is there a method or tool that could elevate your culinary creations even further?

Thinking about these possibilities brings a buzz of excitement. The next section will dive into advanced techniques and features of Traeger grilling, revealing insights that could turn your backyard cookouts into unforgettable dining experiences. Get ready to dig deeper and discover the full potential of your grill, as this journey is just getting started, with endless opportunities ahead. Stay tuned, because what's coming next might just change the way you think about grilling.

USING YOUR TRAEGER GRILL: SETUP AND COOKING MODES

Tip

Always use a heavy-duty, outdoor-rated extension cord if your Traeger grill isn't close to a power outlet. This ensures a steady power supply and helps prevent electrical issues during grilling. Also, keep your wood pellets dry and stored in a sealed container—moisture can cause feeding problems and affect the smoky flavor you want. These small steps make a big difference in both safety and the quality of your grilling results.

First, find the perfect spot for your Traeger grill. Look for a flat, stable surface to keep it from wobbling while you cook, which can mess with your grilling game.

Make sure there's good ventilation so smoke doesn't sneak into your home or bother your neighbors. Also, keep it at least 10 feet away from any structures or overhangs for safety and to give yourself some room to move around while cooking.

Once you've picked the spot, put the grill together following the manufacturer's instructions. It's important to make sure everything is securely fastened because loose parts can cause problems down the line. Check that the grill grates, drip tray, and grease bucket are all working properly, and keep a screwdriver and a wrench handy in case you need to tighten any bolts or screws.

Next up, connect the grill to a power source. Since Traeger grills run on electricity, you'll want to make sure the outlet is working well to avoid any hiccups when you start grilling. If you're using an extension cord, go for a **heavy-duty** one that's rated for outdoor use to ensure a steady power supply.

Now, let's talk about the wood pellets, which are key for that delicious smoky flavor in your food. Fill the hopper with your chosen pellets, making sure they're dry and free from any debris. Wet or dirty pellets can cause feeding issues and make it tough to get the fire going, so store them in a cool, dry place to keep them in top shape.

With the hopper filled, turn on the grill by flipping the power switch to **'ON'** and open the lid to let out any excess smoke during ignition. Once it's powered up, set the temperature dial to the **'Smoke'** setting. This kicks off the heating of the pellets through the grill's hot rod, creating smoke and igniting the fire.

Let the grill preheat for about **10-15 minutes**, and keep an eye on the digital display to see when it hits the right temperature. This preheating step is super important because it ensures the grill is ready for whatever you're cooking. Whether you're slow-cooking a brisket or searing a steak, starting with a properly preheated grill makes a big difference in the final result.

Once your Traeger grill is preheated, dive into the different cooking modes and temperature controls that can really amp up your grilling game. It has several cooking modes, each tailored for specific techniques. Whether you're in the mood for a slow, smoky cook or a quick, high-heat sear, getting the hang of these settings is key.

Start with the **'Smoke'** mode, which is fantastic for giving your food that rich, smoky flavor. It runs at a lower temperature, usually around 180°F, letting the wood pellets smolder and create that signature taste. This mode is great for indirect cooking, where the smoke wraps around your food, enhancing its natural flavors without rushing things. Just remember, patience pays off—the slow infusion of smoke can really elevate your ingredients.

When you need to crank up the heat, switch to the **'High'** mode, which bumps the temperature up to between 400°F and 450°F. This setting is perfect for searing steaks or getting that crispy skin on chicken. The high heat triggers the *Maillard reaction*, giving you a beautifully charred outside while keeping the inside juicy and tender, making your dishes even more delicious.

The digital control panel is your best friend for managing these temperatures. With just a few taps, you can adjust the settings to fit your recipe perfectly. This level of precision is what sets Traeger apart from other grills, letting you keep a consistent heat throughout the cooking process. You can say goodbye to guesswork or constant checking—just set the temperature and let the grill do its thing.

If your model has a built-in meat probe, you're in luck. This handy tool lets you keep an eye on the internal temperature of your food without lifting the lid and losing heat. Just stick the probe into the thickest part of the meat and check the digital display to make sure your food hits that perfect level of doneness, so you avoid overcooking and ensure every bite is packed with flavor.

While you're cooking, keep an eye on the pellet level in the hopper. Running out of pellets mid-cook can throw off both heat and smoke production, which isn't great for your dish. Make it a habit to check and refill the hopper as needed, especially during longer cooking sessions, to keep everything running smoothly and get reliable results every time.

Once your dish is ready, turn the temperature dial to the **'Shutdown Cycle'** to let the grill cool down safely. This important step helps preserve its lifespan and gets it ready for your next cooking adventure, ensuring it's all set when you're ready to fire it up again.

MAINTENANCE MADE SIMPLE

Keeping your Traeger grill in top shape is key to whipping up delicious meals every time. Here's a handy maintenance routine to keep your grill running smoothly and extend its life, so you can wow your family and friends with your grilling prowess.

First up, let's talk about the weekly cleaning routine. After a few uses, grab a heavy-duty wire brush and give those grates a good scrub to get rid of food bits and grease. This not only makes your grill look better but also stops any funky flavors from sneaking into your food. Once the grates are sparkling, don't forget about the grease drip tray and bucket—empty those out to prevent overflow, which can be a fire hazard. A quick wipe down of the outside with a damp cloth and some mild detergent will keep it looking sharp and help fend off rust. This simple routine ensures your grill is always ready to go.

Now, let's dive into the monthly maintenance tasks. The burn pot is super important for performance, and if ash builds up, it can mess things up. Use a shop vacuum to clear out any ash, making sure airflow stays clear for reliable ignition. While you're at it, check the heat baffle and drip tray for any wear or damage, and replace anything that looks iffy. Also, take a peek at the hopper and auger to ensure they're free from pellet dust and debris, which can cause jams and mess with the pellet feed. This monthly check keeps your grill in tip-top shape.

As the seasons shift, it's time for a thorough deep clean. At the start and end of each grilling season, take apart the removable bits like grates, drip trays, and heat baffles. Soak these parts in warm, soapy water, give them a good scrub, and make sure they're completely dry before putting everything back together. While you're doing this, check the electrical connections and power cord for any signs of wear or damage, replacing anything that looks worn out to keep things safe. This seasonal deep clean is crucial for keeping your grill ready for all your cooking adventures.

Regular maintenance checkpoints are also super important. Keep an eye on the **gasket seals** and swap them out if they're looking worn or damaged. This helps keep heat in, which is key for consistent cooking results. Make sure the **chimney cap** and **vents** are clean and clear to allow for optimal smoke flow. Give moving parts, like the hopper lid and grill lid hinges, a little love with food-safe oil to keep them from squeaking and ensure they operate smoothly. These quick checks can really boost performance.

Lastly, let's chat about the best ways to store your pellets. Keep wood pellets in a cool, dry spot, ideally in a sealed container, to stop them from soaking up moisture and going bad. Before each use, check your pellet stash for freshness, since old or damp pellets can mess with performance and the flavor of your food. Keeping your pellets in great shape means every grilling session will be packed with rich, smoky goodness.

TROUBLESHOOTING COMMON TRAEGER GRILL ISSUES

Tip

Always store your Traeger pellets in a sealed, moisture-proof container—even if you only grill on weekends. This simple habit prevents jams, uneven heating, and frustrating cookouts, ensuring your grill is always ready for family gatherings. For extra protection in humid climates, add a small dehumidifier to your storage area. A little prevention goes a long way toward consistent, delicious results and stress-free outdoor cooking.

When you're grilling with a Traeger, one issue you might run into is wet pellets, which are super important for that delicious smoky flavor.

If these pellets soak up moisture, they can cause a bunch of problems. Let's dive into how to spot these pesky pellets and keep your grilling game strong.

First off, you need to know how to identify wet pellets. Keep an eye out for signs like:

- Swollen pellets
- Any weird discoloration
- A musty smell

These are all clues they've absorbed moisture. This can happen if they're left out in the rain or stored somewhere humid. Wet pellets can jam the **auger**, which is the part that feeds them into the firepot, messing up the flow and making it tough to get a good burn. This can lead to uneven heating and temperature control, which is definitely not what you want when you're trying to cook up something tasty.

To keep your pellets in tip-top shape, store them in a sealed, moisture-proof container. You could grab a container made for this purpose or even use a heavy-duty plastic bin with a tight lid. Just make sure it's sturdy enough to handle outdoor conditions if you need it to. If you live in a humid area, tossing a *dehumidifier* in your storage space can really help keep moisture levels down, ensuring your pellets stay dry and ready to go.

If you find wet pellets in your hopper, don't panic—just take some steps to sort it out. Start by emptying the hopper completely and getting rid of all the pellets, even the ones that look dry. It's better to start fresh than risk a jam or uneven burn. After you've emptied it, give the hopper a good clean to remove any dust or debris that could mess with the flow. Once it's all clean, refill it with fresh, dry pellets. Keeping a backup bag handy can really save you if this issue pops up.

Regularly checking on your hopper is key for smooth grilling. Make it a habit to look for any signs of moisture or pellet dust buildup. Over time, dust can accumulate and create blockages that can throw a wrench in your grilling plans. To clean the hopper effectively, use a shop vacuum to suck up any dust or debris—this quick task will help keep everything flowing nicely. Also, don't forget to check the auger to make sure it's clear of any obstructions.

Sticking to these maintenance tasks will really boost your skills with your Traeger grill. Remember, a great grilling experience is all about consistency, and that starts with keeping your pellets dry and your hopper clean. Before you fire up the grill, take a few extra minutes to check on your pellets and hopper. This little bit of diligence will not only improve your grilling results but also help you shine as a backyard grilling pro.

If you're getting some wacky temperature readings on your grill, it's time to take a closer look at those temperature probes. First things first, check the connections to make sure they're snugly plugged into the grill's ports. A loose connection can totally mess with your readings and throw off your cooking game. If everything's connected properly, you can test the probe's accuracy by filling a glass with ice water and sticking it in there; it should read **32°F**. If it's off, try it in boiling water next—your probe should hit **212°F**. If it doesn't, it might be time for a replacement.

Keeping those probes in tip-top shape is super important for getting accurate readings, so make it a habit to clean them after each grilling session. Grease buildup can really throw things off, leading to those annoying fluctuations. Just grab a soft cloth and some mild detergent to wipe them down, making sure they're free of any gunk. If you spot any physical damage or if the readings are still all over the place after a good clean, it's probably best to swap it out for a new one that matches your grill's specs. This way, you'll ensure compatibility and reliability for those perfect grilling moments.

Now, let's talk about those pesky temperature fluctuations. A simple yet effective way to keep things steady is to keep the grill lid closed as much as you can. Every time you lift that lid, you're letting out precious heat, which can lead to instability. So, try to limit how often you peek inside and let your grill do its thing.

Another thing to keep an eye on is the pellet feed and airflow. Make sure the pellets are feeding smoothly into the firepot. Any blockages or hiccups can cause uneven heating, so check the auger for any obstructions and clear them out if needed. Also, ensure that the vents are open and clear to allow proper airflow, which is key for maintaining a consistent temperature while you cook.

If you've tried all this and the fluctuations are still happening, it might be time to check the grill's seals and gaskets. Over time, these can wear out and lead to heat loss. Take a good look at them for any signs of damage, and if they seem worn out, replacing them can really help keep the heat in. This small fix can make a big difference in keeping your cooking temperatures stable.

By fine-tuning these troubleshooting tips, you'll feel more confident and in control of your Traeger grill. But just when you think you've got it all figured out, a new challenge might pop up. Imagine this: you're in the middle of a big family cookout, the grill is going strong, and the mouthwatering smell of steaks fills the air when suddenly, the digital display starts flashing an error code you've never seen before. Panic sets in as you try to figure out what's wrong; is it just a minor glitch, or is there something more serious going on? The pressure is on! What will you do next? Stick around as we dive into the world of error codes and share tips to keep your grill running smoothly, no matter what surprises come your way.

CHAPTER 3

WHAT TO COOK ON YOUR TRAEGER

BEST CUTS OF MEAT FOR SMOKING AND GRILLING

Tip

For busy families aiming to impress, prep your rubs and marinades the night before. This not only saves time on grilling day but also boosts flavor and tenderness. A little planning ahead means you can focus on enjoying your gathering, not just the grill.

When you're getting the hang of grilling and smoking on your Traeger, picking the right cut of beef is super important.
Each cut has its own unique traits that can really make a difference in your results. Let's dive into some of the top choices, starting with brisket.

Brisket is a go-to for barbecue lovers, and it's easy to see why. This cut comes from the lower chest of the cow and is known for its rich marbling and connective tissues. These features make it perfect for smoking because the low and slow cooking lets the fat melt away and the connective tissues break down, resulting in a tender and tasty piece of meat. When you're on the hunt for brisket, go for a whole packer brisket, which includes both the flat and the point; the flat is leaner, while the point is fattier and packed with flavor. Look for a thick flat and a well-defined point to ensure quality, aiming for one that weighs between 10 to 14 pounds for the best smoking experience. Before you smoke it, rub on some salt, pepper, and garlic powder to boost those natural flavors, and smoke it low and slow at about 225°F for around 1 to 1.5 hours per pound until it hits an internal temp of 195°F to 205°F. This method will give you that melt-in-your-mouth goodness.

Next up is the **ribeye**, a cut that shines on the grill and is famous for its marbling and tenderness, making it a crowd-pleaser at any gathering. That marbling not only adds flavor but also helps keep the meat juicy while it cooks. For the best results, go for a bone-in ribeye, as the bone adds extra flavor and moisture. When you're ready to grill, crank up the heat to create a nice sear on the outside while keeping the inside juicy; preheat your grill to about 450°F to 500°F. Season it with salt and pepper, let it come to room temperature, and then throw it on the grill for about 4 to 5 minutes on each side for medium-rare, or until it's cooked to your liking. A meat thermometer is your best friend here—aim for 130°F for medium-rare, and let it rest for a few minutes before serving so those juices can redistribute, making every bite delicious.

Last but not least, we have the **tri-tip**, a versatile cut that works well for both smoking and grilling. It's known for its bold flavor and triangular shape from the bottom sirloin, and it's especially popular on the West Coast but is catching on everywhere. To really amp up the flavor, think about marinating it for a few hours or even overnight. A simple marinade of *olive oil*, *garlic*, *soy sauce*, and a splash of *red wine vinegar* can do wonders. When cooking, aim for medium-rare to keep it tender. If you're grilling, preheat to medium-high heat, around 400°F, and sear each side for about 5 to 7 minutes before moving it to indirect heat to finish cooking until it reaches an internal temp of 130°F to 135°F. If you're smoking it, set your Traeger to 225°F and smoke for about 2 to 3 hours. Once it's done, let it rest for at least 10 minutes before slicing, and make sure to cut against the grain to keep it nice and tender.

Pork shoulder, often called **Boston Butt**, is a must-have for nailing your smoking game. This cut is packed with intramuscular fat and connective tissue, which makes it perfect for creating that tender, flavorful pulled pork we all love. To turn this tough cut into something mouthwatering, you'll want to go low and slow. Fire up your Traeger to a steady 225°F and let it smoke for about 1.5 to 2 hours per pound. This slow cooking helps break down the collagen, so the meat practically falls apart. For an extra flavor boost, rub on a dry mix the night before. A simple blend of:

- 1/4 cup brown sugar
- 2 tablespoons paprika
- 1 tablespoon garlic powder
- 1 tablespoon onion powder
- 1 teaspoon cayenne pepper

Ribs, whether you go for *baby back* or *spare*, are fantastic for grilling and smoking. Baby back ribs are leaner and usually cook up quicker, making them great if you're short on time. On the flip side, spare ribs have more fat, giving them a richer flavor. No matter which you choose, getting juicy ribs takes a bit of prep. Start by peeling off the membrane from the back to help those flavors soak in. Then, slather on your favorite dry rub, making sure to cover every inch. When you're ready to cook, preheat your Traeger to 225°F. Smoke the ribs for about 3 hours, then wrap them in foil with a splash of apple juice or cider to keep them moist before tossing them back on the grill for another 2 hours. Finally, unwrap them, brush on your go-to barbecue sauce, and cook for another hour to let that sauce caramelize. You'll end up with tender, flavorful ribs that will wow your guests.

Tenderloin is another great cut, especially if you need something quick. This lean piece is better for grilling than smoking since it can dry out if you're not careful. To keep it juicy, marinate it for at least an hour before grilling. A simple marinade of:

- 1/4 cup olive oil
- 2 tablespoons lemon juice
- 3 minced garlic cloves
- 1 tablespoon fresh herbs (like rosemary or thyme)

Preheat your grill to medium heat, around 350°F to 400°F, and grill for about 15 to 20 minutes, turning it occasionally until it reaches an internal temp of 145°F. Let it rest for a few minutes before slicing to let those juices redistribute. This quick-cooking cut is perfect for a weeknight dinner or a last-minute get-together.

Trying out these cuts can lead to some seriously tasty results, and don't forget that the type of wood pellets you use can really amp up your pork dishes. For shoulder and ribs, **hickory** or **applewood** pellets are fantastic choices, adding a sweet and smoky flavor that pairs perfectly with the meat. For tenderloin, **cherry** or **pecan** pellets work well for a milder, slightly sweet smoke. Playing around with different pellet flavors can help you find your favorite combos.

Chicken thighs are a great choice for smoking and grilling because they have a bit more fat, which keeps them juicy and flavorful. When you're picking out thighs, go for **bone-in, skin-on** pieces to really amp up the taste and texture. For smoking, fire up your Traeger to about **225°F** and let those thighs cook for **1.5 to 2 hours**. This low-and-slow approach lets the fat render down, giving you tender, juicy meat. If you're grilling instead, preheat your grill to medium heat, around **350°F**, and cook the thighs for about **6 to 8 minutes** on each side. This way, you'll get that crispy skin while keeping the meat nice and moist. A simple mix of salt, pepper, and a hint of *garlic powder* can really bring out the natural flavors without being too overpowering.

Whole chicken is another fantastic option for smoking, as it gives you a mix of textures and flavors from different parts of the bird. To make sure it cooks evenly, think about **spatchcocking** it—basically, you remove the backbone and flatten the chicken. This technique helps it cook uniformly and cuts down on the overall cooking time. Before you smoke it, brine the chicken for at least **4 hours** or even overnight in a mix of water, salt, sugar, and your favorite *herbs*. This step helps keep it moist and adds flavor. Set your Traeger to **225°F** and smoke the chicken for about **3 to 4 hours**, or until it hits an internal temperature of **165°F**. You'll end up with beautifully smoked chicken that has crispy skin and juicy meat.

Lamb shoulder really shines when smoked because of its rich flavor and good fat content, making it perfect for slow cooking. Whip up a rub with herbs like *rosemary*, *thyme*, garlic powder, salt, and pepper. Slather that rub on generously and let it sit for at least **an hour** to soak in the flavors. Set your Traeger to **225°F** and smoke the shoulder for about **6 to 8 hours**, or until it reaches an internal temperature of **195°F**. This slow cooking breaks down the connective tissues, giving you a tender, flavorful piece of meat that practically melts in your mouth.

Lamb chops are perfect for grilling since they cook up quickly and have a tender texture. Just season them with salt, pepper, and a drizzle of *olive oil*. Preheat your grill to high heat, around **450°F**, and grill the chops for about **3 to 4 minutes** on each side. This will give you a nice caramelized exterior while keeping the inside pink and juicy. For an extra kick of flavor, squeeze a bit of *lemon juice* or sprinkle some fresh herbs like *mint* or *parsley* right before serving.

As you get the hang of these cuts, your confidence in grilling and smoking will definitely grow, even if you run into some unexpected hiccups. Picture this: you're hosting a big backyard bash, the grill is hot, and the mouthwatering smell of perfectly cooked meat is wafting through the air. Suddenly, a storm rolls in, threatening to ruin your well-laid plans. The sky darkens, and the first drops of rain start to fall. Will you adapt and keep the good vibes going, or will the weather throw a wrench in your plans? Stick around as we dive into some strategies to handle those curveballs and keep your grilling game strong, no matter what Mother Nature throws your way.

SMOKING FISH AND SEAFOOD ON THE TRAEGER GRILL

Tip

For perfectly smoked fish and shellfish, always preheat your Traeger and use a digital thermometer to monitor internal temps. Brining adds moisture and flavor, while milder wood pellets like apple or alder keep the smoke from overpowering delicate seafood. These small steps make a big difference when you're grilling for family or friends.

When you're smoking fish on your Traeger, salmon is definitely a standout pick. Its rich, oily texture really soaks up those smoky flavors.

For the best results, go for wild-caught salmon; it has a higher fat content that boosts flavor and keeps it nice and moist while smoking. Start by setting your Traeger to a low temperature, somewhere between 180°F and 200°F. This way, the smoke can really get into the fish without drying it out.

To kick things up a notch and keep the fish from sticking, soak a cedar plank in water for at least an hour before you grill. This helps prevent the plank from catching fire and lets it release a lovely, aromatic smoke that pairs perfectly with the salmon. Once your Traeger is preheated, lay the fish on the cedar plank, skin-side down, and sprinkle it with a mix of salt, pepper, and just a touch of *brown sugar* to bring out its natural sweetness. Smoke it for about **1 to 1.5 hours**, or until it hits an internal temperature of **145°F**. You'll end up with a tender, flavorful piece that's sure to impress your guests.

Now, let's talk about **trout**. It's known for its delicate flavor and makes for another fantastic smoking option. Whole trout can be smoked to get that flaky texture infused with smoky goodness. Before you start, clean and prep the fish by removing any pin bones and giving it a rinse under cold water. Pat it dry with paper towels so the seasoning sticks well. A simple mix of fresh *dill, lemon slices*, and a sprinkle of salt can really elevate the trout's natural flavors.

Set your Traeger to that same low temperature, around **180°F to 200°F**, and place the trout right on the grill grates or use a fish basket for easier handling. Smoke it for about **1 to 1.5 hours**, or until the flesh turns opaque and flakes easily with a fork. The gentle smoke will add a subtle, savory flavor that goes great with the brightness of the lemon and dill.

Mackerel is another great choice, especially since it's packed with fat, which makes it perfect for smoking. Unlike salmon and trout, mackerel does better at a slightly higher smoking temperature, so crank your Traeger up to medium heat, around **225°F to 250°F**. This helps avoid overcooking while still getting that rich, smoky flavor.

Before you smoke it, think about pairing mackerel with a sweet glaze or citrus marinade to balance out its natural richness. A simple glaze made from *honey, soy sauce*, and a splash of *lime juice* can really amp up the flavor. Brush that glaze over the fillets and let them marinate for about **30 minutes** to soak in all those tasty flavors. Once your Traeger is ready, place the mackerel on the grill grates and smoke it for about **1 to 1.5 hours**, or until it's cooked through and flaky. You'll end up with a deliciously smoky dish that's perfect for any occasion.

Shrimp is a fantastic pick for your Traeger grill because it cooks up super fast and is really versatile. To get them ready for smoking or grilling, just thread the shrimp onto skewers. This way, they won't slip through the grates, and flipping them becomes a breeze. For a tasty marinade, mix together:

- **1/4 cup** of olive oil
- the juice of **one lemon**
- 3 minced garlic cloves
- **1 tablespoon** of finely chopped fresh herbs like *parsley* or *cilantro*

Let those shrimp soak in the marinade for about **30 minutes** to really amp up the flavor before you cook them.

Set your Traeger to a high temp of around **400°F** for smoking. This helps the shrimp cook quickly while keeping them juicy and tender. Pop the skewers right on the grill grates and smoke them for about **5 to 7 minutes**, turning them once halfway through. You'll know they're done when they turn a bright pink and feel firm to the touch. That high heat and short cooking time really lock in the flavors, giving you a delicious bite.

Oysters are another shellfish that love a hint of smokiness. Start by shucking them, making sure to keep that briny liquid inside the shells. Preheat your Traeger to **225°F** and grab some wood chips like *hickory* or *apple* for a nice, mild smoke flavor. Place the oysters directly on the grill grates, keeping them level so the liquid doesn't spill out, and smoke them for about **20 to 30 minutes**, or until the edges start to curl a bit.

When it's time to serve, a splash of hot sauce or a squeeze of lemon can really brighten up those smoky flavors. A key tip for smoking oysters is to make sure your grill is fully preheated to prevent sticking and keep the temperature steady while cooking. This really enhances their natural briny taste and makes for a unique and tasty appetizer that's perfect for any get-together.

Scallops, with their delicate texture, are better off grilled than smoked. To prep them, pat them dry with paper towels to get rid of any excess moisture—this is crucial for that nice caramelized crust. Just season them lightly with salt, pepper, and a drizzle of olive oil to let their natural sweetness shine. Preheat your Traeger to a high heat of around **450°F** for a quick sear.

Place the scallops right on the grill grates and sear them for about **2 to 3 minutes** on each side. They're ready to flip when they release easily from the grates and have a lovely golden-brown crust. If you're feeling adventurous, you could try a quick smoking session before grilling to add an extra layer of flavor. Just a few minutes at a lower temp of around **225°F** can give them a subtle smokiness without overpowering their delicate taste.

When you're trying out these shellfish options on your Traeger, remember that paying attention to the details is key. Choosing the right marinade and hitting that perfect cooking temperature are essential steps for creating a dish that stands out. Whether you're hosting a laid-back family dinner or throwing an impressive backyard bash, these techniques will help you nail the art of grilling and smoking shellfish, making sure your guests will be coming back for more.

Brining is a key technique for boosting the flavor and moisture of fish when you're smoking it on your Traeger. A good brine can really elevate your final dish. To whip up a basic brine, just mix:

-   one gallon of water
-   one cup of kosher salt
-   half a cup of granulated sugar

This simple mix is a great starting point, but feel free to jazz it up with some herbs or spices like *bay leaves*, *black peppercorns*, or *garlic*. The brining time can vary depending on how thick your fish or seafood is; for thinner fillets like trout, about 30 minutes should do the trick, while thicker cuts like salmon might need up to an hour. Keep an eye on the clock, though—too long in the brine can make your fish way too salty.

Once you've brined your fish, picking the right wood pellets can really amp up the flavor of your smoked dish. For the best results, go for milder wood varieties that enhance the fish's natural taste without overpowering it. **Alder, apple**, and **cherry** wood pellets are fantastic choices, adding a nice touch of sweetness that works well with delicate fish. Steer clear of stronger woods like **mesquite**, as they can drown out the flavor. If you're feeling adventurous, try mixing different types of pellets to create a unique flavor profile that suits your taste.

Keeping the temperature in check is super important for successful smoking. You want to maintain a steady temperature to ensure even cooking and prevent your fish from drying out. Set your Traeger to a low range of 180°F to 200°F for a gentle smoke. A digital thermometer is your best friend here; aim for an internal temperature of at least 145°F to make sure it's fully cooked and safe to eat. Keep an eye on the vents and pellet feed, adjusting as needed to keep that heat steady. It takes a bit of practice, but you'll get the hang of it.

Imagine your fish is perfectly brined, the Traeger is humming along, and the sweet smell of *applewood* smoke is wafting through the air. Then, out of nowhere, dark clouds roll in, and a strong gust of wind shakes the trees. You rush to check the grill, only to see the temperature swinging wildly. As the rain starts to fall, you're faced with a tough choice: do you brave the elements to protect your meal, or do you retreat and hope for the best? The tension is real, and the success of your carefully planned cookout hangs in the balance. With the storm picking up, think about how you can shield your grilling efforts from the unpredictable weather.

GRILLED VEGETABLES, BREADS, AND CREATIVE SIDES

Tip

For perfectly grilled veggies, always dry them thoroughly after washing—excess moisture leads to steaming, not charring. Use a grill basket for small items like cherry tomatoes or mushrooms to prevent them from falling through the grates. Marinate your veggies for at least 30 minutes to maximize flavor, and remember to preheat your Traeger to the right temperature for each type. These small steps make a big difference in taste and texture, ensuring your grilled sides impress every guest.

When you're ready to grill some veggies on your Traeger, the first thing you want to do is pick out a mix that'll really amp up the flavor and texture of your meal.

Bell peppers, zucchini, asparagus, eggplant, and corn are all fantastic options, each bringing something special to the table that grilling can really enhance.

Start by giving those veggies a good wash under running water to get rid of any dirt or pesticides—this is key for keeping things safe to eat. Once they're clean, dry them off well with a kitchen towel or some paper towels. You want to avoid excess moisture because that can lead to steaming instead of grilling, which means you might miss out on that delicious charred flavor and texture.

Next up, chop the veggies into uniform pieces so they cook evenly. For bell peppers, slice them into strips about half an inch wide. Zucchini can be cut into rounds or planks, each around a quarter-inch thick. Don't forget to trim the woody ends off the asparagus, keeping just the tender stalks, and slice the eggplant into rounds or cubes, aiming for about half an inch thick. If you're grilling corn, it's best to keep it on the cob, but you can cut it into smaller sections if that's your style.

For smaller veggies like *cherry tomatoes* or *mushrooms*, grab a grill basket to keep them from slipping through the grates. This handy tool lets air flow while making sure those delicate items soak up all that smoky goodness.

Now, let's talk **marinades** and **seasonings**—they're super important for bringing out those natural flavors. Start with a good splash of high-quality **olive oil**, which helps prevent sticking and adds a nice fruity flavor. From there, feel free to get creative with herbs and spices. If you're in the mood for a Mediterranean vibe, toss in some fresh herbs like thyme, rosemary, or basil, along with minced garlic and a squeeze of fresh lemon juice to really brighten things up.

If you like a bit of heat, consider adding some smoked paprika or chipotle powder for that smoky kick. Let those veggies marinate for at least 30 minutes before grilling; this is crucial for letting the flavors really sink in.

When it's time to fire up the grill, preheat your Traeger to a medium-high temperature, around 375°F. This is perfect for getting that nice char without burning anything. Spread the veggies out in a single layer on the grill to help them cook evenly.

For quick-cooking veggies like asparagus and bell peppers, place them right over the heat source and keep an eye on them, turning occasionally to get that even char.

For denser veggies like eggplant or potatoes, use indirect heat so they cook through without burning on the outside. Position these away from the direct heat source to make sure they get nice and tender all the way through.

While you're grilling, turn the veggies from time to time to get a balanced char and avoid burning. You're aiming for that perfect mix of tenderness and a little crispness, all with a hint of smokiness. Just keep an eye on the grilling times, as they can vary based on the size and type of veggie.

With these tips in your back pocket, you're all set to grill veggies like a pro on your Traeger, and there's still a whole world of non-meat grilling to explore!

For a truly memorable grilling experience, let's dive into some fun techniques for grilling bread and pizza on your Traeger. Start with a rustic loaf or **ciabatta**, slicing it into thick pieces about an inch wide. Give each slice a generous brush with a mix of high-quality **olive oil** and finely minced **garlic**. This not only keeps the bread from sticking to the grill but also fills the air with a delicious, savory aroma. Preheat your Traeger to **375°F**, then pop those slices right on the grill grates. Grill them for about 2 to 3 minutes on each side until you see those lovely grill marks and the outside gets nice and crispy while the inside stays soft.

Now, let's talk pizza. Whether you're using homemade dough or store-bought, roll it out to your favorite thickness—around a quarter-inch usually works well for a balanced crust. Pre-cook the dough on the grill for about 3 to 4 minutes at **450°F**, using a pizza stone to help with even heat and a crispy crust. Once the base is looking good, it's time to add your toppings. Spread a layer of *pesto*, sprinkle on some crumbled *goat cheese*, and toss in roasted veggies like bell peppers and zucchini. Slide the pizza back onto the grill for another 5 to 7 minutes until the cheese is all melted and bubbly, giving you a gourmet creation with a smoky flavor that's sure to wow your guests.

If you're looking for non-meat options, grilled portobello mushrooms are a fantastic alternative to traditional burgers. Marinate those mushrooms in a mix of **balsamic vinegar**, **olive oil**, minced **garlic**, and a pinch of **thyme**, letting them soak up those flavors for at least 30 minutes. Preheat your Traeger to **400°F** and grill the mushrooms for about 5 to 7 minutes on each side until they're tender and juicy. Serve them on a toasted bun with your favorite toppings for a satisfying meal.

Another great non-meat choice is **halloumi cheese**, which is perfect for grilling thanks to its high melting point. Slice the cheese into half-inch thick pieces and give them a light brush with olive oil before grilling at **375°F** for about 2 to 3 minutes per side until they're golden and crispy. Pair it with grilled veggies or toss it into a fresh salad for a deliciously unique dish.

And don't forget about fruits and desserts! Grilling fruits like pineapple, peaches, or watermelon really brings out their natural sweetness. Just cut them into thick slices and grill at **350°F** for about 3 to 4 minutes per side. A drizzle of honey or *balsamic reduction* can really take the flavors up a notch. For a fun dessert, grill slices of pound cake for about 2 minutes per side until they're warm and slightly crispy, then top with grilled fruit and a scoop of vanilla ice cream for a delightful finish to your meal.

As you refine these techniques, think about the setting: the sun setting, the grill sizzling, and the aroma of your culinary creations wafting through the air. Just as you're about to serve your dish, a sudden gust of wind threatens to mess up your carefully arranged table, and the sky darkens while you hear the distant rumble of thunder signaling an approaching storm. Will you be able to protect your culinary triumph from the weather, or will nature have other plans? Stay tuned as we tackle how to handle these unexpected challenges and keep your grilling game strong, no matter what surprises come your way.

CHAPTER 4

PELLET PAIRINGS AND SMOKE SCIENCE

UNDERSTANDING WOOD PELLETS

When it comes to mastering the art of grilling with a Traeger, getting to know wood pellets is key. These little powerhouses are the heart of your grill, providing the heat and flavor that take your outdoor cooking to the next level.

So, let's dive into how they work and why they're so important for nailing your grilling game.

Wood pellets are the main fuel source for your Traeger grill, fed into the firepot by an **auger**, which is just a fancy way of saying a mechanical device that keeps the supply steady and controlled. Once those pellets hit the firepot, they ignite and burn, creating smoke and heat that swirl around the grill, giving your food those delicious, savory flavors. This setup allows for precise temperature control, whether you're going for a low-and-slow smoke at about 225°F or cranking it up to a high-heat sear at 450°F. This flexibility is a big reason why Traeger grills are a hit with both newbies and seasoned pros.

Now, let's talk about how these pellets are made. It all starts with sawdust and wood shavings from hardwoods like oak, hickory, and maple. These materials are dried to a specific moisture level, usually between 5-10%, which is super important for a good burn. After drying, the wood gets ground into a fine powder. Then, under high pressure, it's compressed into those dense pellets, and the heat from this process activates the lignin in the wood, which acts like a natural glue to hold everything together—no chemicals needed. This results in uniform pellets that help you grill consistently.

The quality of your pellets can really make or break your grilling experience. Top-notch options are made from 100% natural hardwoods, ensuring a clean burn with minimal ash. Too much ash can lead to uneven burning and might even damage your grill, while lower-quality pellets might have fillers or additives that mess with your food's flavor and performance. Keeping the size and moisture content consistent is crucial for stable temperatures and getting the cooking results you want.

When picking pellets, it's also important to think about **flavor profiles** since different woods bring unique tastes to your food. For example, *hickory* gives a strong, smoky flavor that pairs perfectly with red meats, while fruitwoods like *apple* or *cherry* offer a milder, sweeter smoke that works great with poultry and pork. Getting to know these flavor characteristics helps you choose the right pellets to boost your recipes and overall taste experience.

Storing your pellets properly is essential for keeping their quality intact. Make sure to keep them in a cool, dry place, ideally in an airtight container, to avoid moisture absorption and degradation. If pellets soak up moisture, they can swell and break apart, leading to problems like auger jams and uneven heating. It's also a good idea to regularly clean your grill's hopper and auger system to prevent pellet dust buildup, ensuring everything feeds smoothly and works reliably.

In the world of Traeger grilling, wood pellets aren't just fuel; they're a crucial ingredient in creating tasty, memorable meals. Understanding how they work, how they're made, and why quality matters will help you up your grilling skills. So, the next time you fire up your Traeger, take a moment to appreciate the role of wood pellets and how they contribute to your grilling success.

FLAVOR PAIRINGS BY PROTEIN

Tip

For busy grillers aiming to impress, try prepping a few different pellet types before your gathering. Mixing woods—like apple with hickory for turkey or cherry with pecan for chicken—lets you easily tailor flavors to each protein. This simple step saves time and ensures every dish has a unique, crowd-pleasing taste. Keep a small selection of pellets on hand, and experiment with blends to discover your family's favorites. Your guests will notice the difference!

When you're firing up the Traeger, getting the flavor pairings just right is key to turning your backyard cookouts into something special.

Let's dive into some wood pellet pairings for red meats and poultry, and see how choosing the right pellets can really amp up your grilling game.

For beef, you want those bold flavors to match its rich profile. **Hickory** pellets are a top pick here, known for their strong, smoky vibe that goes perfectly with cuts like brisket and ribs. This combo really brings out the meat's natural flavors, creating a savory experience that's hard to beat. If you're after a more intense smoke flavor, **mesquite** pellets are your go-to. They pack a punch with their earthy smoke, making them great for bold cuts like tri-tip or flank steak, especially when you want that smoke to shine through. On the flip side, **oak** pellets offer a medium smoke level that works wonders for steaks and roasts, giving a subtle smokiness that enhances the beef's natural flavors without taking over, letting the meat truly shine.

When it comes to pork, the sweet and fruity notes of **apple** and **cherry** wood pellets are a match made in heaven.

- Apple pellets bring a mild, sweet smoke that complements pork's natural sweetness, making them perfect for chops, ribs, and tenderloin. The gentle smoke from apple wood enhances the meat's flavor without overpowering it, leading to a balanced taste experience.
- Cherry pellets kick it up a notch with a slightly stronger fruity smoke, which not only boosts flavor but also adds a rich color to the meat, making them a fantastic choice for ribs and tenderloin, where looks matter just as much as taste.
- If you like a hint of sweetness, **maple** pellets add a subtle, sweet undertone that pairs beautifully with bacon and ham, enriching their natural flavors and adding a nice layer of complexity.

For chicken, lighter woods like **apple**, **cherry**, and **pecan** are the way to go.

- Apple and cherry pellets give off a mild, sweet smoke that complements chicken's delicate flavor, making them ideal for grilling whole birds or wings. The gentle smoke from these woods enhances the meat's natural taste without overwhelming it, resulting in a juicy, flavorful dish.

- Pecan pellets, with their richer, nutty notes, offer a unique flavor profile that's perfect for those looking to add a little depth to their chicken dishes, giving your meal a twist that's sure to impress.

When you're cooking turkey, a mix of **apple** and **hickory** pellets works wonders. The apple brings a sweet, mild smoke that enhances the meat's natural flavors, while the hickory adds depth and complexity, creating a well-rounded flavor profile that elevates both the meat and the skin. This combo results in a turkey that's juicy, flavorful, and sure to steal the show at your holiday table.

As you experiment with these pairings, keep in mind that balance is key for successful grilling. The right wood pellet can really elevate the natural flavors of your protein, making for a dish that's not just tasty but also memorable. Fire up your Traeger, choose your pellets wisely, and get ready to wow your family and friends with your grilling skills. Now, let's take these ideas and apply them to other proteins and dishes, ensuring every meal you grill is a culinary win.

When it comes to fish, picking the right pellets can really amp up the flavor of your catch. **Alder pellets** are fantastic for oily fish like salmon and trout, giving off a light, slightly sweet smoke that brings out their natural richness without drowning out their unique flavors. If you're grilling milder white fish like cod or tilapia, **maple pellets** are a solid pick. Their gentle sweetness pairs perfectly with those subtle tastes, creating a balanced dish that's sure to wow your guests.

Shellfish, with their natural sweetness, also shine with the right pellet pairings. **Alder pellets** boost the sweetness of shrimp, lobster, and scallops, making every bite a treat. If you're looking to add a touch of fruitiness to your seafood, **cherry pellets** bring a nice flavor that works beautifully with shellfish, taking your grilling game up a notch.

When it comes to game meats like venison and duck, you'll want bold flavors to match. **Mesquite pellets** deliver a strong, earthy smoke that complements the rich, gamey taste. If you love a pronounced smokiness, mesquite is your go-to, while **hickory pellets** offer a deep smokiness that enhances these meats, creating a satisfying and memorable meal.

For veggies, **pecan** and **maple pellets** are a match made in heaven. Pecan pellets add a sweet, nutty smoke that really brings out the flavors of peppers, zucchini, and mushrooms. Those nutty notes add a nice complexity to grilled veggies, making them a standout side. Maple pellets, with their mild sweetness, are perfect for root veggies like carrots and sweet potatoes, as the smoke caramelizes their natural sugars for a finish that's hard to resist.

As you play around with these pairings, keep in mind that balance is key for great grilling. The right pellet can really elevate the natural flavors of your proteins or veggies, leading to dishes that are not just tasty but also unforgettable. So fire up your Traeger, choose your pellets wisely, and get ready to impress your family and friends with your grilling skills!

STORING AND HANDLING PELLETS

Tip

For busy grillers, keeping your Traeger pellets in top condition is all about smart storage. Use airtight containers, store them off the ground, and add desiccant packs during humid weather. Regularly check for moisture or mold, and always use the oldest pellets first. These simple habits save you time, prevent grill issues, and ensure every cookout delivers that signature Traeger flavor—so you can focus on enjoying great food and good company.

When you're firing up your Traeger, keeping those wood pellets in top shape is key to getting that consistent, tasty cook every time.

Here are some handy tips to make sure they stay dry and ready to deliver the perfect smoke whenever you light the grill.

First off, where you stash those pellets really matters. You want to keep them in a cool, dry spot to avoid any moisture sneaking in. Too much moisture can lead to swelling, crumbling, and even cause uneven heating or auger jams. So, steer clear of damp places like basements or spots near washing machines. Instead, go for a well-ventilated area that stays dry, like a garage or a dedicated storage shed that won't get damp.

Next up, think about how you store them. The goal is to keep moisture out, and **airtight containers** are your best bet. Heavy-duty plastic bins with snug lids do a great job of blocking humidity and keeping things fresh. If you're buying in bulk and planning for the long haul, *vacuum-sealed bags* are a smart choice. Just make sure those bags are sealed tight to keep air and moisture at bay.

Another important tip is to avoid putting your containers directly on the ground. Storing them right on the floor can lead to moisture transfer, especially if the floor is concrete or tends to be damp. Elevate your storage using:

- pallets
- shelves
- platforms

This little tweak can really help keep your pellets dry and safe from any water damage.

Regular check-ups are a must for keeping quality in check. Make it a habit to inspect your pellets every now and then for any signs of moisture or mold. They should feel firm and dry to the touch. If you spot any that are swollen, soft, or discolored, it's best to toss them. Regular inspections help you avoid contamination and ensure you're only using top-notch pellets in your grill.

When you're buying pellets, try to get amounts that match how often you grill. This way, you minimize storage time and cut down on moisture exposure. Use the **"first in, first out"** method to make sure you're using older pellets first, keeping everything fresh. Keep track of when you bought them and store the newer ones separately from the older ones to avoid any mix-ups.

Weather can be a bit unpredictable, so during those wet or humid days, take some extra precautions. Toss some *desiccant packs* in your storage containers to soak up any extra moisture. If you're grilling in damp conditions, keep your pellets covered until you're ready to use them. This helps keep them dry and ensures they perform at their best.

Transporting pellets also needs a bit of care. Use sealed containers to shield them from rain or humidity while you're on the move, and make sure those containers are secure to prevent spills or exposure to the elements. A little prep goes a long way in keeping your pellets in great shape.

If your pellets accidentally get wet, don't stress. Just spread them out on a dry surface and let them air dry completely before using them. But if they're really soaked or damaged, it's better to replace them to keep your grill's performance up to par.

BONUS EXTRA!!!
Scan to Claim Your Free BBQ Bonuses Now

As SPAM Filters Are Pretty Crazy These Days...
WHITELIST this Email Address:
contact@flamecraftpress.com

In This Way, Your Bonus Will Appear in the Main Folder of Your INBOX and They Will Not Be Buried Along With Other Advertisements in Your PROMOTION/SPAM Folder.

HERE IS HOW TO DO IT:
From Android Smartphone/Tablet
Open the Contacts App;
In the lower right corner, tap + (Add);
Enter **contact@flamecraftpress.com** and then tap Save.

From iPhone/iPad
Open the Contacts App;
In the upper right corner, tap + (Add);
Enter **contact@flamecraftpress.com** and then tap Finish.

THANK YOU FOR YOUR SUPPORT!

I'm eager to know what you think!

Simply scan this QR code to jump straight to my book's review page on Amazon.

Your insights are invaluable – they aid in my growth as an author and assist others in discovering this book.

Feel free to share a photo or video review showcasing you with the book. Your experience could inspire others to embark on their adventure with my book!

Tucker McCoy

CHAPTER 5

RECIPES

BEEF RECIPES

FOR THE TRAEGER GRILL

1. Smoked Beef Short Ribs

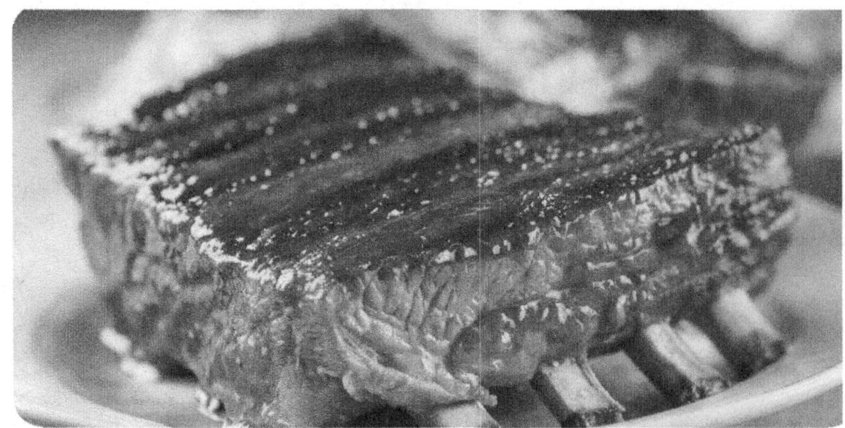

Cooking Time:

5.5-6.5 hours

Preparation Time:

20 minutes

Number of Servings:

4-6

Difficulty Rating:

Medium

INGREDIENTS

- 4 pounds beef short ribs, bone-in
- 1/4 cup kosher salt
- 1/4 cup freshly ground black pepper
- 2 tablespoons smoked paprika
- 2 tablespoons garlic powder
- 1 tablespoon onion powder
- 1 tablespoon brown sugar
- 1 cup beef broth
- 1/2 cup apple cider vinegar
- 1/2 cup BBQ sauce of your choice

DIRECTIONS

1. Preheat your Traeger grill to 225°F with the lid closed for about 15 minutes.

2. In a small bowl, mix together the kosher salt, black pepper, smoked paprika, garlic powder, onion powder, and brown sugar.

3. Pat the short ribs dry with paper towels and generously rub the spice mixture all over the ribs, ensuring even coverage.

4. Place the short ribs directly on the grill grates, bone side down. Insert the probe into the thickest part of one of the ribs, avoiding the bone.

5. Smoke the ribs for 3 hours, maintaining a consistent temperature of 225°F.

6. In a spray bottle, combine the beef broth and apple cider vinegar. Spritz the ribs every hour to keep them moist.

7. After 3 hours, remove the ribs from the grill and wrap them tightly in aluminum foil.

8. Return the wrapped ribs to the grill and continue cooking for an additional 2-3 hours, or until the internal temperature reaches 200°F.

9. Carefully unwrap the ribs and brush them with BBQ sauce.

10. Increase the grill temperature to 275°F and cook the ribs for another 30 minutes to set the sauce.

11. Remove the ribs from the grill and let them rest for 15 minutes before serving.

Rest time: 15 minutes — Traeger settings: Temperature: 225°F, then 275°F Super Smoke: On Probe Use: Yes — Recommended pellets: Hickory — Pro tips: For a richer flavor, consider marinating the ribs overnight in a mixture of beef broth, apple cider vinegar, and spices. — Suggested sides: Potato salad, grilled corn on the cob, or coleslaw — Nutritional facts (per serving): Calories: 700 Protein: 50g Carbohydrates: 15g Fat: 50g Saturated Fat: 20g Cholesterol: 180mg Sodium: 1400mg

2. Grilled Flank Steak with Chimichurri

Cooking Time:

12-16 minutes

Preparation Time:

15 minutes

Number of Servings:

4-6

Difficulty Rating:

Easy

INGREDIENTS

- 2 pounds flank steak
- 1 teaspoon kosher salt
- 1 teaspoon freshly ground black pepper
- 1 tablespoon olive oil
- 1 cup fresh parsley, finely chopped
- 1/2 cup fresh cilantro, finely chopped
- 1/4 cup red wine vinegar
- 3 cloves garlic, minced
- 1 teaspoon crushed red pepper flakes
- 1/2 cup olive oil
- Salt and pepper to taste

DIRECTIONS

1. Preheat your Traeger grill to 450°F with the lid closed for about 15 minutes.

2. Pat the flank steak dry with paper towels. Season both sides with kosher salt and freshly ground black pepper.

3. Drizzle olive oil over the steak, ensuring an even coating.

4. Place the flank steak directly on the grill grates. Insert the probe into the thickest part of the steak.

5. Grill the steak for 6-8 minutes per side, or until the internal temperature reaches 130°F for medium-rare.

6. While the steak is grilling, prepare the chimichurri sauce. In a medium bowl, combine parsley, cilantro, red wine vinegar, minced garlic, and crushed red pepper flakes. Slowly whisk in olive oil until well combined. Season with salt and pepper to taste.

7. Once the steak reaches the desired temperature, remove it from the grill and let it rest for 10 minutes.

8. Slice the steak thinly against the grain and serve with chimichurri sauce drizzled on top.

Rest time: 10 minutes — Traeger settings: Temperature: 450°F Super Smoke: Off Probe Use: Yes — Recommended pellets: Mesquite — Pro tips: For extra flavor, marinate the flank steak in olive oil, garlic, and herbs for at least 2 hours before grilling. — Suggested sides: Grilled vegetables, garlic bread, or a fresh garden salad — Nutritional facts (per serving): Calories: 350 Protein: 30g Carbohydrates: 2g Fat: 25g Saturated Fat: 5g Cholesterol: 70mg Sodium: 400mg

3. Traeger Smoked Prime Rib

Cooking Time:

3-4 hours

Preparation Time:

20 minutes

Number of Servings:

6-8

Difficulty Rating:

Medium

INGREDIENTS

- 5 pounds prime rib roast, bone-in
- 1/4 cup kosher salt
- 1/4 cup freshly ground black pepper
- 2 tablespoons garlic powder
- 2 tablespoons onion powder
- 1 tablespoon dried rosemary
- 1 tablespoon dried thyme
- 1/4 cup olive oil
- 1/4 cup Dijon mustard

DIRECTIONS

1. Preheat your Traeger grill to 250°F with the lid closed for about 15 minutes.

2. In a small bowl, mix together the kosher salt, black pepper, garlic powder, onion powder, dried rosemary, and dried thyme.

3. Pat the prime rib roast dry with paper towels. Rub the olive oil all over the roast, then coat it with the Dijon mustard.

4. Generously apply the spice mixture to the entire surface of the roast, pressing it in to ensure it adheres well.

5. Place the prime rib directly on the grill grates, bone side down. Insert the probe into the thickest part of the roast, avoiding the bone.

6. Smoke the prime rib for 3-4 hours, or until the internal temperature reaches 125°F for medium-rare.

7. Once the desired temperature is reached, remove the roast from the grill and let it rest for 20 minutes before carving.

Rest time: 20 minutes — Traeger settings: Temperature: 250°F Super Smoke: On Probe Use: Yes — Recommended pellets: Oak — Pro tips: For an extra layer of flavor, consider dry-aging the prime rib in your refrigerator for 3-5 days before cooking. — Suggested sides: Garlic mashed potatoes, roasted asparagus, or a Caesar salad — Nutritional facts (per serving): Calories: 800 Protein: 60g Carbohydrates: 5g Fat: 60g Saturated Fat: 25g Cholesterol: 200mg Sodium: 1500mg

4. BBQ Beef Back Ribs

Cooking Time:

5 hours 30 minutes

Preparation Time:

20 minutes

Number of Servings:

4-6

Difficulty Rating:

Medium

INGREDIENTS

- 4 pounds beef back ribs
- 1/4 cup kosher salt
- 1/4 cup freshly ground black pepper
- 2 tablespoons smoked paprika
- 2 tablespoons garlic powder
- 1 tablespoon onion powder
- 1 tablespoon brown sugar
- 1 teaspoon cayenne pepper
- 1 cup apple cider vinegar
- 1 cup apple juice
- 1 cup BBQ sauce

DIRECTIONS

1. Preheat your Traeger grill to 225°F with the lid closed for about 15 minutes.

2. In a small bowl, mix together the kosher salt, black pepper, smoked paprika, garlic powder, onion powder, brown sugar, and cayenne pepper.

3. Pat the beef back ribs dry with paper towels. Generously rub the spice mixture all over the ribs, ensuring an even coating.

4. Place the ribs directly on the grill grates, bone side down. Insert the probe into the thickest part of the meat, avoiding the bone.

5. Smoke the ribs for 3 hours.

6. In a spray bottle, combine the apple cider vinegar and apple juice. Spritz the ribs every hour to keep them moist.

7. After 3 hours, remove the ribs from the grill and wrap them tightly in aluminum foil. Return them to the grill and continue cooking for another 2 hours.

8. Unwrap the ribs and brush them with BBQ sauce. Place them back on the grill for an additional 30 minutes to set the sauce.

9. Once the internal temperature reaches 200°F, remove the ribs from the grill and let them rest for 10 minutes before serving.

Rest time: 10 minutes — Traeger settings: Temperature: 225°F Super Smoke: On Probe Use: Yes — Recommended pellets: Hickory — Pro tips: For extra tenderness, marinate the ribs in apple juice overnight before applying the rub. — Suggested sides: Coleslaw, baked beans, or cornbread — Nutritional facts (per serving): Calories: 700 Protein: 50g Carbohydrates: 20g Fat: 50g Saturated Fat: 20g Cholesterol: 150mg Sodium: 1200mg

5. Grilled Beef Kebabs with Vegetables

Cooking Time:

10-12 minutes

Preparation Time:

20 minutes

Number of Servings:

4-6

Difficulty Rating:

Easy

INGREDIENTS

- 2 pounds beef sirloin, cut into 1-inch cubes
- 1 red bell pepper, cut into 1-inch pieces
- 1 yellow bell pepper, cut into 1-inch pieces
- 1 red onion, cut into wedges
- 1 zucchini, sliced into 1/2-inch rounds
- 1/4 cup olive oil
- 2 tablespoons soy sauce
- 2 tablespoons Worcestershire sauce
- 1 tablespoon garlic powder
- 1 tablespoon onion powder
- 1 teaspoon smoked paprika
- 1 teaspoon black pepper
- 1 teaspoon kosher salt
- 8-10 metal or soaked wooden skewers

DIRECTIONS

1. Preheat your Traeger grill to 400°F with the lid closed for about 15 minutes.

2. In a large bowl, combine olive oil, soy sauce, Worcestershire sauce, garlic powder, onion powder, smoked paprika, black pepper, and kosher salt. Mix well to create the marinade.

3. Add the beef cubes to the marinade, ensuring they are well coated. Let them marinate for at least 30 minutes, or up to 2 hours for more flavor.

4. Thread the marinated beef cubes, bell peppers, red onion, and zucchini onto the skewers, alternating between meat and vegetables.

5. Place the skewers directly on the grill grates. Grill for 10-12 minutes, turning occasionally, until the beef reaches your desired level of doneness and the vegetables are tender.

6. Remove the skewers from the grill and let them rest for 5 minutes before serving.

Rest time: 5 minutes — Traeger settings: Temperature: 400°F Super Smoke: Off Probe Use: No — Recommended pellets: Mesquite — Pro tips: For added flavor, try marinating the beef overnight in the refrigerator. — Suggested sides: Grilled corn on the cob, potato salad, or a fresh garden salad — Nutritional facts (per serving): Calories: 350 Protein: 30g Carbohydrates: 10g Fat: 20g Saturated Fat: 5g Cholesterol: 80mg Sodium: 800mg

6. Smoked Beef Chuck Roast

Cooking Time:

6-7 hours

Preparation Time:

15 minutes

Number of Servings:

6-8

Difficulty Rating:

Medium

INGREDIENTS

- 5 pounds beef chuck roast
- 2 tablespoons kosher salt
- 2 tablespoons freshly ground black pepper
- 1 tablespoon garlic powder
- 1 tablespoon onion powder
- 1 tablespoon smoked paprika
- 1 teaspoon dried thyme
- 1 teaspoon dried rosemary
- 1/2 cup beef broth
- 1/4 cup apple cider vinegar
- 1/4 cup Worcestershire sauce

DIRECTIONS

1. Preheat your Traeger grill to 225°F with the lid closed for about 15 minutes.

2. In a small bowl, mix together the kosher salt, black pepper, garlic powder, onion powder, smoked paprika, thyme, and rosemary.

3. Pat the beef chuck roast dry with paper towels. Generously rub the spice mixture all over the roast, ensuring an even coating.

4. Place the roast directly on the grill grates. Insert the probe into the thickest part of the meat.

5. Smoke the roast for 3 hours.

6. In a small bowl, combine the beef broth, apple cider vinegar, and Worcestershire sauce.

7. After 3 hours, remove the roast from the grill and place it in a large aluminum foil pan. Pour the liquid mixture over the roast.

8. Cover the pan tightly with aluminum foil and return it to the grill. Continue cooking for another 3-4 hours, or until the internal temperature reaches 200°F.

9. Remove the roast from the grill and let it rest for 20 minutes before slicing.

Rest time: 20 minutes — Traeger settings: Temperature: 225°F Super Smoke: On Probe Use: Yes — Recommended pellets: Oak — Pro tips: For added flavor, marinate the roast overnight in the refrigerator with the spice rub. — Suggested sides: Mashed potatoes, roasted vegetables, or a fresh green salad — Nutritional facts (per serving): Calories: 600 Protein: 50g Carbohydrates: 5g Fat: 40g Saturated Fat: 15g Cholesterol: 150mg Sodium: 1200mg

7. Traeger Grilled T-Bone Steak

Cooking Time:

12-14 minutes

Preparation Time:

10 minutes

Number of Servings:

2-4

Difficulty Rating:

Easy

INGREDIENTS

- 2 T-bone steaks, about 1.5 inches thick
- 2 tablespoons olive oil
- 2 teaspoons kosher salt
- 2 teaspoons freshly ground black pepper
- 1 tablespoon garlic powder
- 1 tablespoon onion powder
- 1 teaspoon smoked paprika
- 1 teaspoon dried thyme

DIRECTIONS

1. Preheat your Traeger grill to 450°F with the lid closed for about 15 minutes.

2. In a small bowl, mix together the kosher salt, black pepper, garlic powder, onion powder, smoked paprika, and dried thyme.

3. Pat the T-bone steaks dry with paper towels. Brush both sides with olive oil.

4. Generously season both sides of the steaks with the spice mixture, pressing it into the meat to ensure it adheres well.

5. Place the steaks directly on the grill grates. Insert the probe into the thickest part of one of the steaks, avoiding the bone.

6. Grill the steaks for 6-7 minutes per side, or until the internal temperature reaches 130°F for medium-rare. Adjust the time as needed for your preferred level of doneness.

7. Remove the steaks from the grill and let them rest for 10 minutes before serving.

Rest time: 10 minutes — Traeger settings: Temperature: 450°F Super Smoke: Off Probe Use: Yes — Recommended pellets: Hickory — Pro tips: For an extra layer of flavor, try adding a pat of herb butter on top of the steaks during the last minute of grilling. — Suggested sides: Grilled asparagus, baked potatoes, or a Caesar salad — Nutritional facts (per serving): Calories: 700 Protein: 60g Carbohydrates: 2g Fat: 50g Saturated Fat: 20g Cholesterol: 180mg Sodium: 1200mg

8. Smoked Beef Tri-Tip

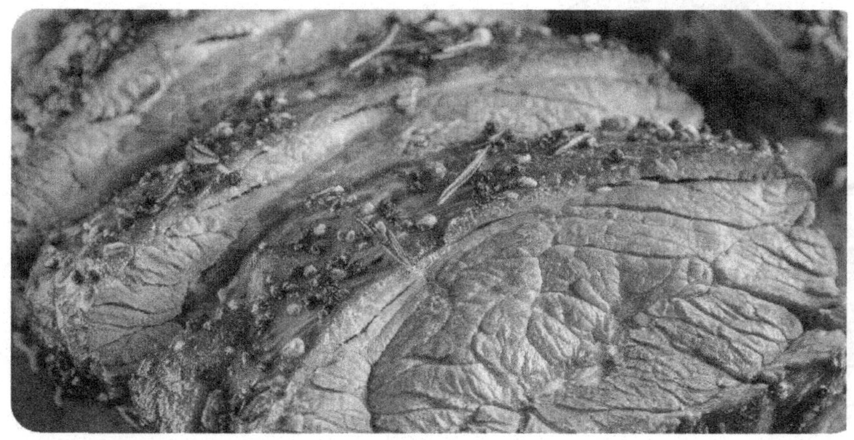

Cooking Time:

2-3 hours

Preparation Time:

10 minutes

Number of Servings:

4-6

Difficulty Rating:

Medium

INGREDIENTS

- 2.5 pounds beef tri-tip roast
- 2 tablespoons olive oil
- 2 teaspoons kosher salt
- 2 teaspoons freshly ground black pepper
- 1 tablespoon garlic powder
- 1 tablespoon onion powder
- 1 teaspoon smoked paprika
- 1 teaspoon dried rosemary

DIRECTIONS

1. Preheat your Traeger grill to 225°F with the lid closed for about 15 minutes.

2. In a small bowl, mix together the kosher salt, black pepper, garlic powder, onion powder, smoked paprika, and dried rosemary.

3. Pat the tri-tip roast dry with paper towels. Brush all sides with olive oil.

4. Generously season the tri-tip with the spice mixture, pressing it into the meat to ensure it adheres well.

5. Place the tri-tip directly on the grill grates. Insert the probe into the thickest part of the meat.

6. Smoke the tri-tip for 2-3 hours, or until the internal temperature reaches 130°F for medium-rare. Adjust the time as needed for your preferred level of doneness.

7. Remove the tri-tip from the grill and let it rest for 15 minutes before slicing against the grain.

Rest time: 15 minutes — Traeger settings: Temperature: 225°F Super Smoke: On Probe Use: Yes — Recommended pellets: Mesquite — Pro tips: For a deeper flavor, marinate the tri-tip overnight in the refrigerator with the spice rub. — Suggested sides: Grilled corn on the cob, coleslaw, or garlic bread — Nutritional facts (per serving): Calories: 450 Protein: 40g Carbohydrates: 3g Fat: 30g Saturated Fat: 12g Cholesterol: 110mg Sodium: 800mg

9. Grilled Beef Burgers with Cheddar

Cooking Time:

10-12 minutes

Preparation Time:

10 minutes

Number of Servings:

4

Difficulty Rating:

Easy

INGREDIENTS

- 2 pounds ground beef (80/20 blend)
- 1 teaspoon kosher salt
- 1 teaspoon freshly ground black pepper
- 1 tablespoon Worcestershire sauce
- 4 slices sharp cheddar cheese
- 4 hamburger buns
- 1 tablespoon olive oil
- Optional toppings: lettuce, tomato slices, red onion slices, pickles, ketchup, mustard

DIRECTIONS

1. Preheat your Traeger grill to 400°F with the lid closed for about 15 minutes.

2. In a large bowl, combine the ground beef, kosher salt, black pepper, and Worcestershire sauce. Mix gently with your hands until just combined. Avoid over-mixing to keep the burgers tender.

3. Divide the mixture into 4 equal portions and shape each into a patty about ¾ inch thick. Make a slight indentation in the center of each patty with your thumb to prevent puffing up during cooking.

4. Brush the grill grates with olive oil to prevent sticking.

5. Place the patties directly on the grill grates. Insert the probe into the center of one of the patties.

6. Grill the burgers for 5-6 minutes per side, or until the internal temperature reaches 160°F for medium doneness.

7. During the last minute of grilling, place a slice of cheddar cheese on each patty and close the lid to melt the cheese.

8. Remove the burgers from the grill and let them rest for 5 minutes.

9. Toast the hamburger buns on the grill for about 1 minute, until lightly browned.

10. Assemble the burgers with your choice of toppings and serve immediately.

Rest time: 5 minutes — Traeger settings: Temperature: 400°F Super Smoke: Off Probe Use: Yes — Recommended pellets: Oak — Pro tips: For an extra burst of flavor, try adding a slice of crispy bacon on top of the cheese before serving. — Suggested sides: Sweet potato fries, coleslaw, or a garden salad — Nutritional facts (per serving): Calories: 650 Protein: 40g Carbohydrates: 30g Fat: 40g Saturated Fat: 18g Cholesterol: 120mg Sodium: 900mg

10. Smoked Beef Meatloaf

Cooking Time:

2-3 hours

Preparation Time:

15 minutes

Number of Servings:

6-8

Difficulty Rating:

Medium

INGREDIENTS

- 2 pounds ground beef (80/20 blend)
- 1 cup breadcrumbs
- 1/2 cup whole milk
- 1/2 cup finely chopped onion
- 2 cloves garlic, minced
- 2 large eggs
- 1 tablespoon Worcestershire sauce
- 1 teaspoon kosher salt
- 1 teaspoon freshly ground black pepper
- 1/2 cup ketchup
- 1 tablespoon brown sugar
- 1 teaspoon smoked paprika

DIRECTIONS

1. Preheat your Traeger grill to 225°F with the lid closed for about 15 minutes.

2. In a large bowl, combine the breadcrumbs and milk. Let them soak for about 5 minutes until the breadcrumbs absorb the milk.

3. Add the ground beef, chopped onion, minced garlic, eggs, Worcestershire sauce, kosher salt, and black pepper to the breadcrumb mixture. Mix gently with your hands until just combined. Avoid over-mixing to keep the meatloaf tender.

4. Shape the mixture into a loaf about 9 inches long and 4 inches wide. Place it on a piece of parchment paper or a grill-safe baking dish.

5. In a small bowl, mix together the ketchup, brown sugar, and smoked paprika. Spread half of this glaze over the top of the meatloaf.

6. Place the meatloaf on the grill grates, using the parchment paper or baking dish. Insert the probe into the center of the meatloaf.

7. Smoke the meatloaf for 2-3 hours, or until the internal temperature reaches 160°F.

8. During the last 30 minutes of cooking, spread the remaining glaze over the meatloaf.

9. Remove the meatloaf from the grill and let it rest for 10 minutes before slicing.

Rest time: 10 minutes — Traeger settings: Temperature: 225°F Super Smoke: On Probe Use: Yes — Recommended pellets: Hickory — Pro tips: For a deeper flavor, prepare the meatloaf mixture a day in advance and let it rest in the refrigerator overnight. — Suggested sides: Mashed potatoes, green beans, or a fresh garden salad — Nutritional facts (per serving): Calories: 450 Protein: 30g Carbohydrates: 20g Fat: 30g Saturated Fat: 12g Cholesterol: 110mg Sodium: 850mg

11. Traeger Grilled Beef Skewers

Cooking Time:

10-12 minutes

Preparation Time:

15 minutes

Number of Servings:

4-6

Difficulty Rating:

Easy

INGREDIENTS

- 2 pounds beef sirloin, cut into 1-inch cubes
- 1/4 cup olive oil
- 2 tablespoons soy sauce
- 1 tablespoon Worcestershire sauce
- 1 tablespoon honey
- 2 cloves garlic, minced
- 1 teaspoon kosher salt
- 1 teaspoon freshly ground black pepper
- 1 red bell pepper, cut into 1-inch pieces
- 1 green bell pepper, cut into 1-inch pieces
- 1 red onion, cut into 1-inch pieces
- 8-10 wooden skewers, soaked in water for 30 minutes

DIRECTIONS

1. In a large bowl, whisk together olive oil, soy sauce, Worcestershire sauce, honey, minced garlic, kosher salt, and black pepper.

2. Add the beef cubes to the marinade, tossing to coat evenly. Cover and refrigerate for at least 1 hour, or up to 4 hours for more flavor.

3. Preheat your Traeger grill to 400°F with the lid closed for about 15 minutes.

4. Thread the marinated beef, bell peppers, and onion pieces onto the soaked skewers, alternating between meat and vegetables.

5. Place the skewers directly on the grill grates. Insert the probe into the center of one of the beef cubes.

6. Grill the skewers for 10-12 minutes, turning occasionally, until the internal temperature of the beef reaches 135°F for medium-rare doneness.

7. Remove the skewers from the grill and let them rest for 5 minutes before serving.

Rest time: 5 minutes — Traeger settings: Temperature: 400°F Super Smoke: Off Probe Use: Yes — Recommended pellets: Mesquite — Pro tips: For extra flavor, try adding a sprinkle of your favorite dry rub to the beef before grilling. — Suggested sides: Grilled corn on the cob, potato salad, or a fresh garden salad — Nutritional facts (per serving): Calories: 450 Protein: 35g Carbohydrates: 15g Fat: 30g Saturated Fat: 10g Cholesterol: 90mg Sodium: 800mg

12. Smoked Beef Jerky

Cooking Time:

4-5 hours

Preparation Time:

15 minutes

Number of Servings:

8-10

Difficulty Rating:

Medium

INGREDIENTS

- 2 pounds beef eye of round, trimmed of fat and sliced into 1/4-inch thick strips
- 1/2 cup soy sauce
- 1/4 cup Worcestershire sauce
- 2 tablespoons brown sugar
- 1 tablespoon smoked paprika
- 1 teaspoon garlic powder
- 1 teaspoon onion powder
- 1 teaspoon freshly ground black pepper
- 1/2 teaspoon cayenne pepper (optional, for heat)
- 1/2 teaspoon kosher salt

DIRECTIONS

1. In a large bowl, combine soy sauce, Worcestershire sauce, brown sugar, smoked paprika, garlic powder, onion powder, black pepper, cayenne pepper, and kosher salt. Whisk until the sugar is dissolved and the mixture is well combined.

2. Add the beef strips to the marinade, ensuring each piece is well coated. Cover the bowl with plastic wrap and refrigerate for at least 4 hours, or overnight for maximum flavor.

3. Preheat your Traeger grill to 180°F with the lid closed for about 15 minutes.

4. Remove the beef strips from the marinade, allowing any excess to drip off. Discard the marinade.

5. Arrange the beef strips directly on the grill grates, leaving space between each piece for even smoking.

6. Smoke the beef jerky for 4-5 hours, or until the jerky is dry but still slightly pliable. Check periodically to ensure it doesn't over-dry.

7. Remove the jerky from the grill and let it cool completely on a wire rack before storing.

Rest time: None — Traeger settings: Temperature: 180°F Super Smoke: On Probe Use: No — Recommended pellets: Hickory or Mesquite — Pro tips: For best results, slice the beef against the grain for a more tender jerky. Store the cooled jerky in an airtight container or vacuum-sealed bag to maintain freshness. — Suggested sides: Serve with a variety of nuts and dried fruits for a perfect snack platter. — Nutritional facts (per serving): Calories: 150 Protein: 25g Carbohydrates: 5g Fat: 3g Saturated Fat: 1g Cholesterol: 50mg Sodium: 800mg

PORK RECIPES
FOR THE TRAEGER GRILL

13. Smoked Pork Belly Burnt Ends

Cooking Time:

4-5 hours

Preparation Time:

15 minutes

Number of Servings:

6-8

Difficulty Rating:

Medium

INGREDIENTS

- 3 pounds pork belly, skin removed, cut into 1.5-inch cubes
- 1/4 cup yellow mustard
- 1/4 cup brown sugar
- 2 tablespoons paprika
- 1 tablespoon garlic powder
- 1 tablespoon onion powder
- 1 tablespoon kosher salt
- 1 teaspoon freshly ground black pepper
- 1/2 cup barbecue sauce
- 1/4 cup honey
- 1/4 cup apple juice

DIRECTIONS

1. In a small bowl, combine brown sugar, paprika, garlic powder, onion powder, kosher salt, and black pepper to create a dry rub.

2. Pat the pork belly cubes dry with paper towels. Rub the mustard all over the pork, then generously apply the dry rub, ensuring each cube is well coated.

3. Preheat your Traeger grill to 250°F with the lid closed for about 15 minutes.

4. Place the pork belly cubes directly on the grill grates, ensuring they are spaced apart for even cooking.

5. Smoke the pork belly for 2.5 to 3 hours, or until they develop a nice bark and are tender.

6. In a disposable aluminum pan, combine barbecue sauce, honey, and apple juice. Add the smoked pork belly cubes to the pan and toss to coat them in the sauce mixture.

7. Cover the pan with aluminum foil and return it to the grill. Cook for an additional 1.5 to 2 hours, or until the pork belly is tender and the sauce has caramelized.

8. Remove the pan from the grill and let the pork belly rest for 10 minutes before serving.

Rest time: 10 minutes — Traeger settings: Temperature: 250°F Super Smoke: On Probe Use: No — Recommended pellets: Hickory or Cherry — Pro tips: For an extra layer of flavor, let the seasoned pork belly sit in the refrigerator overnight before smoking. — Suggested sides: Macaroni and cheese, coleslaw, or baked beans — Nutritional facts (per serving): Calories: 700 Protein: 20g Carbohydrates: 30g Fat: 60g Saturated Fat: 22g Cholesterol: 80mg Sodium: 800mg

14. Grilled Pork Loin with Herb Rub

Cooking Time:

1.5-2 hours

Preparation Time:

15 minutes

Number of Servings:

6-8

Difficulty Rating:

Medium

INGREDIENTS

- 1 (3-4 pound) boneless pork loin
- 3 tablespoons olive oil
- 2 tablespoons kosher salt
- 1 tablespoon freshly ground black pepper
- 2 tablespoons garlic powder
- 1 tablespoon onion powder
- 1 tablespoon dried rosemary
- 1 tablespoon dried thyme
- 1 tablespoon dried sage
- 1 tablespoon lemon zest

DIRECTIONS

1. Preheat your Traeger grill to 350°F with the lid closed for about 15 minutes.

2. In a small bowl, combine kosher salt, black pepper, garlic powder, onion powder, rosemary, thyme, sage, and lemon zest to create the herb rub.

3. Pat the pork loin dry with paper towels. Rub it with olive oil, then generously apply the herb rub, ensuring the entire surface is covered.

4. Place the pork loin directly on the grill grates. Insert the probe into the thickest part of the loin.

5. Grill the pork loin for 1.5 to 2 hours, or until the internal temperature reaches 145°F.

6. Remove the pork loin from the grill and let it rest for 10 minutes before slicing and serving.

Rest time: 10 minutes — Traeger settings: Temperature: 350°F Super Smoke: Off Probe Use: Yes — Recommended pellets: Apple or Maple — Pro tips: For a more intense flavor, let the pork loin sit with the herb rub in the refrigerator for a few hours before grilling. — Suggested sides: Grilled asparagus, mashed potatoes, or a Caesar salad — Nutritional facts (per serving): Calories: 350 Protein: 40g Carbohydrates: 2g Fat: 20g Saturated Fat: 5g Cholesterol: 120mg Sodium: 800mg

15. Smoked Pork Shoulder with Carolina Sauce

Cooking Time:

8-10 hours

Preparation Time:

20 minutes

Number of Servings:

10-12

Difficulty Rating:

Medium

INGREDIENTS

- 1 (8-10 pound) bone-in pork shoulder
- 1/4 cup yellow mustard
- 1/4 cup apple cider vinegar
- 1/4 cup brown sugar
- 2 tablespoons paprika
- 2 tablespoons kosher salt
- 1 tablespoon garlic powder
- 1 tablespoon onion powder
- 1 tablespoon freshly ground black pepper
- 1 teaspoon cayenne pepper
- 1 cup apple juice
- 1 cup Carolina-style barbecue sauce

DIRECTIONS

1. In a small bowl, combine brown sugar, paprika, kosher salt, garlic powder, onion powder, black pepper, and cayenne pepper to create a dry rub.

2. Pat the pork shoulder dry with paper towels. Rub the mustard all over the pork, then generously apply the dry rub, ensuring the entire surface is well coated.

3. Preheat your Traeger grill to 225°F with the lid closed for about 15 minutes.

4. Place the pork shoulder directly on the grill grates, fat side up. Insert the probe into the thickest part of the shoulder, avoiding the bone.

5. Smoke the pork shoulder for 8 to 10 hours, or until the internal temperature reaches 195°F. Spritz the pork with apple juice every hour to keep it moist.

6. Once the pork reaches the desired temperature, remove it from the grill and let it rest for 30 minutes.

7. Shred the pork using two forks, discarding any excess fat. Toss the shredded pork with Carolina-style barbecue sauce before serving.

Rest time: 30 minutes — Traeger settings: Temperature: 225°F Super Smoke: On Probe Use: Yes — Recommended pellets: Hickory or Apple — Pro tips: For deeper flavor, let the seasoned pork shoulder sit in the refrigerator overnight before smoking. — Suggested sides: Cornbread, coleslaw, or potato salad — Nutritional facts (per serving): Calories: 500 Protein: 40g Carbohydrates: 15g Fat: 30g Saturated Fat: 10g Cholesterol: 120mg Sodium: 900mg

16. Traeger Grilled Pork Ribs with Dry Rub

Cooking Time:

6 hours

Preparation Time:

20 minutes

Number of Servings:

4-6

Difficulty Rating:

Medium

INGREDIENTS

- 2 racks of pork ribs (about 3-4 pounds each)
- 1/4 cup yellow mustard
- 1/4 cup apple cider vinegar
- 1/4 cup brown sugar
- 2 tablespoons paprika
- 2 tablespoons kosher salt
- 1 tablespoon garlic powder
- 1 tablespoon onion powder
- 1 tablespoon freshly ground black pepper
- 1 teaspoon cayenne pepper
- 1/2 cup apple juice

DIRECTIONS

1. In a small bowl, combine brown sugar, paprika, kosher salt, garlic powder, onion powder, black pepper, and cayenne pepper to create a dry rub.

2. Pat the ribs dry with paper towels. Rub the mustard all over the ribs, then generously apply the dry rub, ensuring the entire surface is well coated.

3. Preheat your Traeger grill to 225°F with the lid closed for about 15 minutes.

4. Place the ribs directly on the grill grates, bone side down. Insert the probe into the thickest part of the meat, avoiding the bone.

5. Smoke the ribs for 3 hours.

6. After 3 hours, remove the ribs from the grill and wrap them tightly in aluminum foil with apple juice. Return them to the grill and cook for an additional 2 hours.

7. Unwrap the ribs and place them back on the grill for 1 more hour to allow the bark to firm up.

8. Once the ribs are tender and the internal temperature reaches 195°F, remove them from the grill and let them rest for 15 minutes before slicing and serving.

Rest time: 15 minutes — Traeger settings: Temperature: 225°F Super Smoke: On Probe Use: Yes — Recommended pellets: Hickory or Cherry — Pro tips: For extra flavor, let the seasoned ribs sit in the refrigerator overnight before smoking. — Suggested sides: Baked beans, coleslaw, or cornbread — Nutritional facts (per serving): Calories: 600 Protein: 45g Carbohydrates: 20g Fat: 40g Saturated Fat: 15g Cholesterol: 150mg Sodium: 1000mg

17. Smoked Bacon-Wrapped Pork Medallions

Cooking Time:

1 hour

Preparation Time:

15 minutes

Number of Servings:

4

Difficulty Rating:

Easy

INGREDIENTS

- 1 pound pork tenderloin, cut into 1-inch medallions
- 12 slices of bacon
- 1 tablespoon olive oil
- 1 tablespoon brown sugar
- 1 teaspoon smoked paprika
- 1 teaspoon garlic powder
- 1 teaspoon onion powder
- 1 teaspoon kosher salt
- 1/2 teaspoon freshly ground black pepper
- Toothpicks

DIRECTIONS

1. Preheat your Traeger grill to 225°F with the lid closed for about 15 minutes.

2. In a small bowl, combine brown sugar, smoked paprika, garlic powder, onion powder, kosher salt, and black pepper to create a seasoning mix.

3. Pat the pork medallions dry with paper towels. Rub each medallion with olive oil, then generously apply the seasoning mix, ensuring all sides are well coated.

4. Wrap each pork medallion with a slice of bacon, securing it with a toothpick.

5. Place the bacon-wrapped medallions directly on the grill grates. Insert the probe into the center of one of the medallions.

6. Smoke the medallions for 1 hour, or until the internal temperature reaches 145°F.

7. Once the medallions reach the desired temperature, remove them from the grill and let them rest for 5 minutes before serving.

Rest time: 5 minutes — Traeger settings: Temperature: 225°F Super Smoke: On Probe Use: Yes — Recommended pellets: Hickory or Apple — Pro tips: For extra flavor, let the seasoned pork medallions sit in the refrigerator for 30 minutes before wrapping them in bacon. — Suggested sides: Grilled asparagus, mashed potatoes, or a fresh garden salad — Nutritional facts (per serving): Calories: 350 Protein: 30g Carbohydrates: 5g Fat: 25g Saturated Fat: 8g Cholesterol: 80mg Sodium: 700mg

18. Grilled Pork Sausages with Peppers

Cooking Time:

40 minutes

Preparation Time:

15 minutes

Number of Servings:

4

Difficulty Rating:

Easy

INGREDIENTS

- 8 pork sausages
- 2 tablespoons olive oil
- 2 red bell peppers, sliced
- 2 yellow bell peppers, sliced
- 1 large red onion, sliced
- 2 cloves garlic, minced
- 1 teaspoon kosher salt
- 1/2 teaspoon freshly ground black pepper
- 1 teaspoon dried oregano
- 1 teaspoon smoked paprika
- 1/4 cup balsamic vinegar

DIRECTIONS

1. Preheat your Traeger grill to 350°F with the lid closed for about 15 minutes.

2. In a large bowl, combine the sliced bell peppers, red onion, and minced garlic. Drizzle with olive oil and season with kosher salt, black pepper, oregano, and smoked paprika. Toss to coat evenly.

3. Place the seasoned vegetables in a grill-safe pan or cast-iron skillet.

4. Place the pan with vegetables on the grill grates and cook for 15 minutes, stirring occasionally.

5. Add the pork sausages directly onto the grill grates alongside the pan. Grill the sausages for 20-25 minutes, turning occasionally, until they are cooked through and have a nice char.

6. Once the vegetables are tender and slightly caramelized, drizzle them with balsamic vinegar and stir to combine.

7. Remove both the sausages and the vegetable pan from the grill. Let the sausages rest for 5 minutes before serving.

Rest time: 5 minutes — Traeger settings: Temperature: 350°F Super Smoke: Off Probe Use: No — Recommended pellets: Maple or Pecan — Pro tips: For an extra kick, add a pinch of red pepper flakes to the vegetable mix before grilling. — Suggested sides: Crusty bread, potato salad, or a simple green salad — Nutritional facts (per serving): Calories: 450 Protein: 20g Carbohydrates: 25g Fat: 30g Saturated Fat: 10g Cholesterol: 60mg Sodium: 900mg

19. Smoked Pork Loin with Maple Glaze

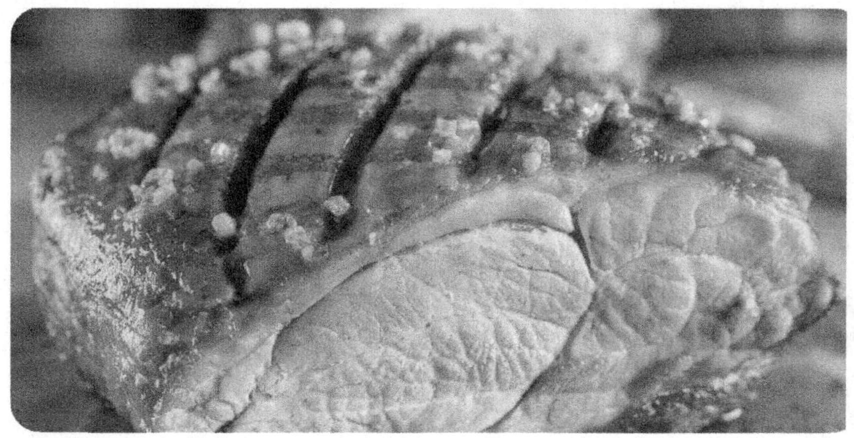

Cooking Time:

2.5 to 3 hours

Number of Servings:

6-8

Preparation Time:

20 minutes

Difficulty Rating:

Medium

INGREDIENTS

- 1 (3-4 pound) boneless pork loin
- 1/4 cup pure maple syrup
- 2 tablespoons Dijon mustard
- 2 tablespoons apple cider vinegar
- 2 tablespoons olive oil
- 2 cloves garlic, minced
- 1 teaspoon kosher salt
- 1/2 teaspoon freshly ground black pepper
- 1/2 teaspoon smoked paprika

DIRECTIONS

1. Preheat your Traeger grill to 225°F with the lid closed for about 15 minutes.

2. In a small bowl, whisk together the maple syrup, Dijon mustard, apple cider vinegar, olive oil, minced garlic, kosher salt, black pepper, and smoked paprika to create the glaze.

3. Pat the pork loin dry with paper towels. Using a sharp knife, score the fat cap in a crosshatch pattern, being careful not to cut into the meat.

4. Brush the pork loin generously with the maple glaze, ensuring all sides are well coated. Reserve some glaze for basting later.

5. Place the pork loin directly on the grill grates. Insert the probe into the thickest part of the meat.

6. Smoke the pork loin for 2.5 to 3 hours, or until the internal temperature reaches 145°F, basting with the reserved glaze every 30 minutes.

7. Once the pork loin reaches the desired temperature, remove it from the grill and let it rest for 10 minutes before slicing and serving.

Rest time: 10 minutes — Traeger settings: Temperature: 225°F Super Smoke: On Probe Use: Yes — Recommended pellets: Maple or Cherry — Pro tips: For a deeper flavor, marinate the pork loin in the glaze for up to 4 hours in the refrigerator before grilling. — Suggested sides: Roasted sweet potatoes, coleslaw, or grilled corn on the cob — Nutritional facts (per serving): Calories: 320 Protein: 35g Carbohydrates: 10g Fat: 15g Saturated Fat: 4g Cholesterol: 100mg Sodium: 450mg

20. Traeger Grilled Pork Skewers with Pineapple

Cooking Time:

12-15 minutes

Preparation Time:

20 minutes

Number of Servings:

4-6

Difficulty Rating:

Easy

INGREDIENTS

- 2 pounds pork tenderloin, cut into 1-inch cubes
- 1 fresh pineapple, peeled, cored, and cut into 1-inch cubes
- 1/4 cup soy sauce
- 1/4 cup honey
- 2 tablespoons olive oil
- 2 tablespoons lime juice
- 2 cloves garlic, minced
- 1 teaspoon kosher salt
- 1/2 teaspoon freshly ground black pepper
- 1/2 teaspoon smoked paprika
- 1/4 teaspoon cayenne pepper (optional)
- 8-10 wooden skewers, soaked in water for 30 minutes

DIRECTIONS

1. In a large bowl, whisk together the soy sauce, honey, olive oil, lime juice, minced garlic, kosher salt, black pepper, smoked paprika, and cayenne pepper.

2. Add the pork cubes to the marinade, tossing to coat evenly. Cover and refrigerate for at least 1 hour, or up to 4 hours for more flavor.

3. Preheat your Traeger grill to 400°F with the lid closed for about 15 minutes.

4. Thread the marinated pork and pineapple cubes alternately onto the soaked skewers, leaving a little space between each piece for even cooking.

5. Place the skewers directly on the grill grates. Grill for 12-15 minutes, turning occasionally, until the pork is cooked through and has a nice char.

6. Remove the skewers from the grill and let them rest for 5 minutes before serving.

Rest time: 5 minutes — Traeger settings: Temperature: 400°F Super Smoke: Off Probe Use: No — Recommended pellets: Hickory or Apple — Pro tips: For extra juiciness, brine the pork cubes in a saltwater solution for 30 minutes before marinating. — Suggested sides: Coconut rice, grilled vegetables, or a fresh green salad — Nutritional facts (per serving): Calories: 350 Protein: 30g Carbohydrates: 25g Fat: 15g Saturated Fat: 4g Cholesterol: 80mg Sodium: 800mg

21. Smoked Pork Chops with Honey Mustard

Cooking Time:

1.5 to 2 hours

Preparation Time:

15 minutes

Number of Servings:

4

Difficulty Rating:

Easy

INGREDIENTS

- 4 bone-in pork chops, about 1 inch thick
- 1/4 cup honey
- 1/4 cup Dijon mustard
- 2 tablespoons apple cider vinegar
- 2 tablespoons olive oil
- 2 cloves garlic, minced
- 1 teaspoon kosher salt
- 1/2 teaspoon freshly ground black pepper
- 1/2 teaspoon smoked paprika

DIRECTIONS

1. Preheat your Traeger grill to 225°F with the lid closed for about 15 minutes.

2. In a small bowl, whisk together the honey, Dijon mustard, apple cider vinegar, olive oil, minced garlic, kosher salt, black pepper, and smoked paprika to create the marinade.

3. Pat the pork chops dry with paper towels. Place them in a large resealable plastic bag or a shallow dish.

4. Pour the marinade over the pork chops, ensuring they are well coated. Seal the bag or cover the dish and refrigerate for at least 1 hour, or up to 4 hours for more flavor.

5. Remove the pork chops from the marinade and let them come to room temperature for about 15 minutes.

6. Place the pork chops directly on the grill grates. Insert the probe into the thickest part of one of the chops.

7. Smoke the pork chops for 1.5 to 2 hours, or until the internal temperature reaches 145°F.

8. Once the pork chops reach the desired temperature, remove them from the grill and let them rest for 5 minutes before serving.

Rest time: 5 minutes — Traeger settings: Temperature: 225°F Super Smoke: On Probe Use: Yes — Recommended pellets: Apple or Cherry — Pro tips: For an extra layer of flavor, add a sprig of fresh rosemary to the marinade. — Suggested sides: Grilled asparagus, mashed potatoes, or a fresh garden salad — Nutritional facts (per serving): Calories: 420 Protein: 35g Carbohydrates: 20g Fat: 22g Saturated Fat: 6g Cholesterol: 110mg Sodium: 600mg

22. Grilled Pork Burgers with Coleslaw

Cooking Time:

12-16 minutes

Preparation Time:

20 minutes

Number of Servings:

6

Difficulty Rating:

Easy

INGREDIENTS

- 2 pounds ground pork
- 1/4 cup breadcrumbs
- 1/4 cup grated Parmesan cheese
- 1 tablespoon Worcestershire sauce
- 1 tablespoon Dijon mustard
- 2 cloves garlic, minced
- 1 teaspoon kosher salt
- 1/2 teaspoon freshly ground black pepper
- 1/2 teaspoon smoked paprika
- 1/4 teaspoon cayenne pepper (optional)
- 6 hamburger buns

DIRECTIONS

1. In a large bowl, combine the ground pork, breadcrumbs, Parmesan cheese, Worcestershire sauce, Dijon mustard, minced garlic, kosher salt, black pepper, smoked paprika, and cayenne pepper. Mix until just combined, being careful not to overwork the meat.

2. Divide the mixture into 6 equal portions and shape each into a patty about 1/2 inch thick.

3. Preheat your Traeger grill to 375°F with the lid closed for about 15 minutes.

4. While the grill is preheating, prepare the coleslaw. In a medium bowl, whisk together the mayonnaise, apple cider vinegar, honey, celery seed, kosher salt, and black pepper. Add the shredded cabbage and carrots, tossing to coat evenly. Set aside.

5. Place the pork patties directly on the grill grates. Grill for 6-8 minutes per side, or until the internal temperature reaches 160°F.

6. During the last 2 minutes of grilling, place the hamburger buns cut side down on the grill to toast lightly.

7. Remove the pork patties and buns from the grill. Let the patties rest for 5 minutes.

8. Assemble the burgers by placing a pork patty on the bottom half of each bun, topping with a generous scoop of coleslaw, and finishing with the top half of the bun.

Coleslaw: 2 cups shredded green cabbage 1 cup shredded carrots 1/4 cup mayonnaise 1 tablespoon apple cider vinegar 1 tablespoon honey 1/2 teaspoon celery seed 1/4 teaspoon kosher salt 1/4 teaspoon freshly ground black pepper — Rest time: 5 minutes — Traeger settings: Temperature: 375°F Super Smoke: Off Probe Use: Yes — Recommended pellets: Hickory or Apple — Pro tips: For added flavor, mix in a tablespoon of your favorite barbecue sauce into the pork mixture before forming the patties. — Suggested sides: Sweet potato fries, grilled corn on the cob, or a fresh fruit salad — Nutritional facts (per serving): Calories: 450 Protein: 28g Carbohydrates: 35g Fat: 22g Saturated Fat: 7g Cholesterol: 90mg Sodium: 850mg

23. Smoked Pork and Beans

Cooking Time:
2.5 to 3 hours

Preparation Time:
20 minutes

Number of Servings:
6

Difficulty Rating:
Medium

INGREDIENTS

- 1 pound pork shoulder, cut into 1-inch cubes
- 2 tablespoons olive oil
- 1 large onion, diced
- 3 cloves garlic, minced
- 1 can (15 ounces) tomato sauce
- 1/4 cup molasses
- 1/4 cup apple cider vinegar
- 2 tablespoons Worcestershire sauce
- 2 tablespoons brown sugar
- 1 tablespoon Dijon mustard
- 1 teaspoon smoked paprika
- 1/2 teaspoon cayenne pepper (optional)
- 1 teaspoon kosher salt
- 1/2 teaspoon freshly ground black pepper
- 2 cans (15 ounces each) navy beans, drained and rinsed
- 1/4 cup chopped fresh parsley for garnish

DIRECTIONS

1. Preheat your Traeger grill to 225°F with the lid closed for about 15 minutes.

2. In a large cast-iron skillet or Dutch oven, heat the olive oil over medium heat. Add the pork cubes and sear on all sides until browned, about 5-7 minutes. Remove the pork and set aside.

3. In the same skillet, add the diced onion and minced garlic. Sauté until the onion is translucent, about 3-4 minutes.

4. Stir in the tomato sauce, molasses, apple cider vinegar, Worcestershire sauce, brown sugar, Dijon mustard, smoked paprika, cayenne pepper, kosher salt, and black pepper. Mix well to combine.

5. Return the pork to the skillet, along with the drained navy beans. Stir to coat everything evenly with the sauce.

6. Place the skillet on the Traeger grill grates. Insert the probe into one of the larger pieces of pork.

7. Smoke the pork and beans for 2.5 to 3 hours, or until the pork is tender and the internal temperature reaches 195°F. Stir occasionally to ensure even cooking.

8. Once done, remove the skillet from the grill and let it rest for 10 minutes. Garnish with chopped fresh parsley before serving.

Rest time: 10 minutes — Traeger settings: Temperature: 225°F Super Smoke: On Probe Use: Yes — Recommended pellets: Hickory or Mesquite — Pro tips: For a deeper flavor, marinate the pork cubes in the sauce mixture for a few hours before cooking. — Suggested sides: Cornbread, coleslaw, or a simple green salad — Nutritional facts (per serving): Calories: 480 Protein: 28g Carbohydrates: 45g Fat: 22g Saturated Fat: 6g Cholesterol: 70mg Sodium: 950mg

24. Traeger Grilled Pork Belly Tacos

Cooking Time:

3 to 3.5 hours

Preparation Time:

20 minutes

Number of Servings:

6

Difficulty Rating:

Medium

INGREDIENTS

- 2 pounds pork belly, skin removed
- 1 tablespoon olive oil
- 1 tablespoon kosher salt
- 1 teaspoon freshly ground black pepper
- 1 teaspoon smoked paprika
- 1 teaspoon garlic powder
- 1 teaspoon onion powder
- 1/2 teaspoon cayenne pepper (optional)
- 12 small corn tortillas
- 1 cup diced pineapple
- 1/2 cup chopped fresh cilantro
- 1/4 cup diced red onion
- 1 lime, cut into wedges

DIRECTIONS

1. Preheat your Traeger grill to 275°F with the lid closed for about 15 minutes.

2. Pat the pork belly dry with paper towels. Rub the olive oil all over the pork belly.

3. In a small bowl, mix together the kosher salt, black pepper, smoked paprika, garlic powder, onion powder, and cayenne pepper. Rub the spice mixture evenly over the pork belly.

4. Place the pork belly directly on the grill grates, fat side up. Insert the probe into the thickest part of the pork belly.

5. Smoke the pork belly for 3 to 3.5 hours, or until the internal temperature reaches 200°F and the meat is tender.

6. Remove the pork belly from the grill and let it rest for 15 minutes.

7. While the pork is resting, warm the corn tortillas on the grill for about 1 minute per side.

8. Slice the pork belly into thin strips.

9. Assemble the tacos by placing a few slices of pork belly on each tortilla. Top with diced pineapple, chopped cilantro, and diced red onion. Serve with lime wedges on the side.

Rest time: 15 minutes — Traeger settings: Temperature: 275°F Super Smoke: On Probe Use: Yes — Recommended pellets: Apple or Cherry — Pro tips: For extra crispy pork belly, increase the grill temperature to 400°F for the last 10 minutes of cooking. — Suggested sides: Mexican street corn, black bean salad, or guacamole — Nutritional facts (per serving): Calories: 550 Protein: 25g Carbohydrates: 40g Fat: 35g Saturated Fat: 12g Cholesterol: 80mg Sodium: 950mg

CHICKEN RECIPES

FOR THE TRAEGER GRILL

25. Smoked Chicken Breasts with Garlic Butter

Cooking Time:

1 hour 30 minutes

Preparation Time:

10 minutes

Number of Servings:

4

Difficulty Rating:

Easy

INGREDIENTS

- 4 boneless, skinless chicken breasts
- 1/4 cup unsalted butter, melted
- 4 cloves garlic, minced
- 1 tablespoon fresh lemon juice
- 1 teaspoon kosher salt
- 1/2 teaspoon freshly ground black pepper
- 1 teaspoon smoked paprika
- 1 tablespoon fresh parsley, chopped

DIRECTIONS

1. Preheat your Traeger grill to 225°F with the lid closed for about 15 minutes.

2. In a small bowl, combine the melted butter, minced garlic, lemon juice, kosher salt, black pepper, and smoked paprika. Mix well.

3. Place the chicken breasts in a large resealable plastic bag or shallow dish. Pour the garlic butter mixture over the chicken, ensuring each breast is well coated. Seal the bag or cover the dish and let it marinate in the refrigerator for at least 1 hour.

4. Remove the chicken from the marinade and let any excess drip off. Discard the marinade.

5. Place the chicken breasts directly on the grill grates. Insert the probe into the thickest part of one of the breasts.

6. Smoke the chicken for 1 hour at 225°F.

7. Increase the grill temperature to 375°F and continue to cook the chicken for an additional 20 to 30 minutes, or until the internal temperature reaches 165°F.

8. Once cooked, remove the chicken from the grill and let it rest for 5 minutes before serving. Garnish with chopped parsley.

Rest time: 5 minutes — Traeger settings: Temperature: 225°F, then 375°F Super Smoke: On Probe Use: Yes — Recommended pellets: Pecan or Alder — Pro tips: For extra flavor, marinate the chicken overnight in the refrigerator. — Suggested sides: Roasted potatoes, steamed asparagus, or a fresh garden salad — Nutritional facts (per serving): Calories: 320 Protein: 35g Carbohydrates: 2g Fat: 20g Saturated Fat: 8g Cholesterol: 120mg Sodium: 600mg

26. Grilled Chicken Drumsticks with Spicy Rub

Cooking Time:

35 to 40 minutes

Preparation Time:

10 minutes

Number of Servings:

4

Difficulty Rating:

Easy

INGREDIENTS

- 12 chicken drumsticks
- 2 tablespoons olive oil
- 1 tablespoon smoked paprika
- 1 tablespoon garlic powder
- 1 tablespoon onion powder
- 1 teaspoon cayenne pepper
- 1 teaspoon kosher salt
- 1/2 teaspoon freshly ground black pepper
- 1/2 teaspoon ground cumin

DIRECTIONS

1. Preheat your Traeger grill to 375°F with the lid closed for about 15 minutes.

2. In a small bowl, combine the smoked paprika, garlic powder, onion powder, cayenne pepper, kosher salt, black pepper, and ground cumin. Mix well to create the spicy rub.

3. Pat the chicken drumsticks dry with paper towels. This helps the rub adhere better and promotes crispy skin.

4. Drizzle the olive oil over the drumsticks and rub it in to coat each piece evenly.

5. Sprinkle the spicy rub over the drumsticks, ensuring each one is thoroughly coated. Use your hands to press the rub into the skin for maximum flavor.

6. Place the drumsticks directly on the grill grates. Insert the probe into the thickest part of one of the drumsticks, avoiding the bone.

7. Grill the drumsticks for 35 to 40 minutes, or until the internal temperature reaches 175°F, turning them halfway through to ensure even cooking.

8. Once cooked, remove the drumsticks from the grill and let them rest for 5 minutes before serving.

Rest time: 5 minutes — Traeger settings: Temperature: 375°F Super Smoke: Off Probe Use: Yes — Recommended pellets: Hickory or Mesquite — Pro tips: For an extra kick, add a pinch more cayenne pepper to the rub. — Suggested sides: Coleslaw, corn on the cob, or baked beans — Nutritional facts (per serving): Calories: 350 Protein: 30g Carbohydrates: 2g Fat: 24g Saturated Fat: 6g Cholesterol: 150mg Sodium: 700mg

27. Traeger Smoked Whole Chicken

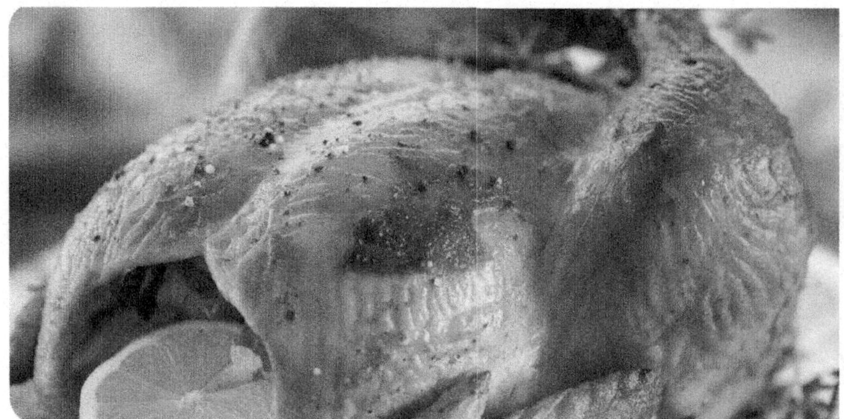

Cooking Time:

2 hours 30 minutes to 2 hours 45 minutes

Preparation Time:

15 minutes

Number of Servings:

4-6

Difficulty Rating:

Medium

INGREDIENTS

- 1 whole chicken (4-5 pounds)
- 2 tablespoons olive oil
- 2 tablespoons kosher salt
- 1 tablespoon freshly ground black pepper
- 1 tablespoon smoked paprika
- 1 tablespoon garlic powder
- 1 tablespoon onion powder
- 1 lemon, halved
- 1 bunch fresh thyme

DIRECTIONS

1. Preheat your Traeger grill to 225°F with the lid closed for about 15 minutes.

2. Pat the chicken dry with paper towels, both inside and out. This helps the seasoning stick and promotes crispy skin.

3. Rub the olive oil all over the chicken, ensuring it is evenly coated.

4. In a small bowl, combine the kosher salt, black pepper, smoked paprika, garlic powder, and onion powder. Mix well.

5. Generously season the chicken inside and out with the spice mixture, making sure to cover all areas.

6. Squeeze the juice of one lemon half inside the cavity of the chicken, then place both lemon halves and the bunch of thyme inside the cavity.

7. Truss the chicken legs with kitchen twine to ensure even cooking.

8. Place the chicken directly on the grill grates, breast side up. Insert the probe into the thickest part of the breast, avoiding the bone.

9. Smoke the chicken at 225°F for 2 hours.

10. Increase the grill temperature to 375°F and continue to cook for an additional 30 to 45 minutes, or until the internal temperature reaches 165°F.

11. Once cooked, remove the chicken from the grill and let it rest for 10 minutes before carving.

Rest time: 10 minutes — Traeger settings: Temperature: 225°F, then 375°F Super Smoke: On Probe Use: Yes — Recommended pellets: Apple or Cherry — Pro tips: For extra flavor, marinate the chicken overnight in the refrigerator with your favorite herbs and spices. — Suggested sides: Grilled vegetables, mashed potatoes, or a Caesar salad — Nutritional facts (per serving): Calories: 450 Protein: 40g Carbohydrates: 2g Fat: 30g Saturated Fat: 8g Cholesterol: 150mg Sodium: 800mg

28. Grilled Chicken Skewers with Vegetables

Cooking Time:

12 to 15 minutes

Preparation Time:

15 minutes

Number of Servings:

4

Difficulty Rating:

Easy

INGREDIENTS

- 1.5 pounds boneless, skinless chicken breasts, cut into 1-inch cubes
- 2 tablespoons olive oil
- 1 tablespoon lemon juice
- 1 tablespoon soy sauce
- 1 tablespoon honey
- 2 cloves garlic, minced
- 1 teaspoon smoked paprika
- 1 teaspoon dried oregano
- 1 teaspoon kosher salt
- 1/2 teaspoon freshly ground black pepper
- 1 red bell pepper, cut into 1-inch pieces
- 1 yellow bell pepper, cut into 1-inch pieces
- 1 red onion, cut into wedges
- 8 wooden skewers, soaked in water for 30 minutes

DIRECTIONS

1. In a large bowl, combine olive oil, lemon juice, soy sauce, honey, minced garlic, smoked paprika, oregano, kosher salt, and black pepper. Whisk until well combined.

2. Add the chicken cubes to the marinade, ensuring each piece is well coated. Cover and refrigerate for at least 30 minutes, or up to 2 hours for more flavor.

3. Preheat your Traeger grill to 400°F with the lid closed for about 15 minutes.

4. Thread the marinated chicken, bell peppers, and onion onto the soaked skewers, alternating between chicken and vegetables.

5. Place the skewers directly on the grill grates. Grill for 12 to 15 minutes, turning occasionally, until the chicken is cooked through and the vegetables are slightly charred. The internal temperature of the chicken should reach 165°F.

6. Remove the skewers from the grill and let them rest for 5 minutes before serving.

Rest time: 5 minutes — Traeger settings: Temperature: 400°F Super Smoke: Off Probe Use: No — Recommended pellets: Maple or Pecan — Pro tips: For added flavor, marinate the chicken overnight. — Suggested sides: Rice pilaf, grilled corn, or a fresh garden salad — Nutritional facts (per serving): Calories: 320 Protein: 35g Carbohydrates: 15g Fat: 14g Saturated Fat: 2g Cholesterol: 95mg Sodium: 600mg

29. Smoked Chicken Quarters with Maple Glaze

Cooking Time:

2 hours to 2 hours 15 minutes

Number of Servings:

4

Preparation Time:

15 minutes

Difficulty Rating:

Medium

INGREDIENTS

- 4 chicken quarters (leg and thigh attached)
- 2 tablespoons olive oil
- 2 teaspoons kosher salt
- 1 teaspoon freshly ground black pepper
- 1 teaspoon smoked paprika
- 1 teaspoon garlic powder
- 1 teaspoon onion powder
- 1/2 cup pure maple syrup
- 2 tablespoons apple cider vinegar
- 1 tablespoon Dijon mustard
- 1/4 teaspoon cayenne pepper (optional)

DIRECTIONS

1. Preheat your Traeger grill to 225°F with the lid closed for about 15 minutes.

2. Pat the chicken quarters dry with paper towels to ensure the seasoning adheres well.

3. Rub olive oil over each chicken quarter, making sure they are evenly coated.

4. In a small bowl, mix together kosher salt, black pepper, smoked paprika, garlic powder, and onion powder.

5. Season the chicken quarters generously with the spice mixture, covering all sides.

6. In a separate bowl, whisk together maple syrup, apple cider vinegar, Dijon mustard, and cayenne pepper (if using) to create the glaze.

7. Place the chicken quarters directly on the grill grates, skin side up. Insert the probe into the thickest part of one of the thighs, avoiding the bone.

8. Smoke the chicken at 225°F for 1.5 hours.

9. Increase the grill temperature to 375°F and brush the chicken with the maple glaze. Continue to cook for an additional 30 to 45 minutes, basting with glaze every 10 minutes, until the internal temperature reaches 175°F.

10. Once cooked, remove the chicken from the grill and let it rest for 10 minutes before serving.

Rest time: 10 minutes — Traeger settings: Temperature: 225°F, then 375°F Super Smoke: On Probe Use: Yes — Recommended pellets: Maple or Hickory — Pro tips: For a deeper flavor, marinate the chicken in the glaze for a few hours before grilling. — Suggested sides: Coleslaw, baked beans, or cornbread — Nutritional facts (per serving): Calories: 520 Protein: 45g Carbohydrates: 20g Fat: 30g Saturated Fat: 8g Cholesterol: 180mg Sodium: 900mg

30. Traeger Grilled Chicken Tenders with Ranch Dip

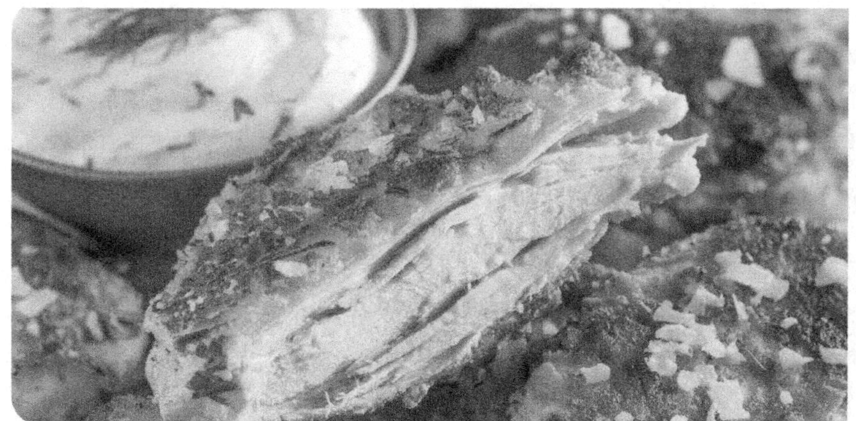

Cooking Time:

20 to 25 minutes

Preparation Time:

20 minutes

Number of Servings:

4

Difficulty Rating:

Easy

INGREDIENTS

- 1.5 pounds chicken tenders
- 2 tablespoons olive oil
- 1 tablespoon apple cider vinegar
- 1 tablespoon Dijon mustard
- 1 teaspoon garlic powder
- 1 teaspoon onion powder
- 1 teaspoon smoked paprika
- 1 teaspoon kosher salt
- 1/2 teaspoon freshly ground black pepper
- 1/2 teaspoon cayenne pepper (optional)
- 1 cup buttermilk
- 1 cup all-purpose flour
- 1 cup panko breadcrumbs
- 1/2 cup grated Parmesan cheese
- 1 tablespoon chopped fresh parsley

DIRECTIONS

1. In a large bowl, combine olive oil, apple cider vinegar, Dijon mustard, garlic powder, onion powder, smoked paprika, kosher salt, black pepper, and cayenne pepper (if using). Whisk until well combined.

2. Add the chicken tenders to the marinade, ensuring each piece is well coated. Cover and refrigerate for at least 30 minutes, or up to 2 hours for more flavor.

3. Preheat your Traeger grill to 375°F with the lid closed for about 15 minutes.

4. In a shallow dish, pour the buttermilk. In another shallow dish, mix together the flour, panko breadcrumbs, and Parmesan cheese.

5. Remove the chicken tenders from the marinade, allowing any excess to drip off. Dip each tender into the buttermilk, then dredge in the breadcrumb mixture, pressing gently to adhere.

6. Place the breaded chicken tenders directly on the grill grates. Grill for 20 to 25 minutes, turning halfway through, until the chicken is golden brown and cooked through. The internal temperature should reach 165°F.

7. While the chicken is grilling, prepare the ranch dip by combining sour cream, mayonnaise, lemon juice, dill, chives, garlic powder, onion powder, kosher salt, and black pepper in a bowl. Mix until smooth and well combined.

8. Remove the chicken tenders from the grill and let them rest for 5 minutes before serving with the ranch dip.

Ranch dip: 1 cup sour cream 1/2 cup mayonnaise 1 tablespoon lemon juice 1 tablespoon chopped fresh dill 1 tablespoon chopped fresh chives 1 teaspoon garlic powder 1 teaspoon onion powder 1/2 teaspoon kosher salt 1/4 teaspoon freshly ground black pepper — Rest time: 5 minutes — Traeger settings: Temperature: 375°F Super Smoke: Off Probe Use: No — Recommended pellets: Hickory or Cherry — Pro tips: For extra crispiness, spray the chicken tenders lightly with cooking spray before grilling. — Suggested sides: Potato wedges, coleslaw, or a fresh green salad — Nutritional facts (per serving): Calories: 450 Protein: 40g Carbohydrates: 30g Fat: 20g Saturated Fat: 6g Cholesterol: 110mg Sodium: 850mg

31. Smoked Chicken Legs with Sweet Chili Sauce

Cooking Time:

2 hours to 2 hours 15 minutes

Preparation Time:

15 minutes

Number of Servings:

4

Difficulty Rating:

Medium

INGREDIENTS

- 8 chicken legs
- 2 tablespoons olive oil
- 2 teaspoons kosher salt
- 1 teaspoon freshly ground black pepper
- 1 teaspoon smoked paprika
- 1 teaspoon garlic powder
- 1 teaspoon onion powder
- 1 cup sweet chili sauce
- 2 tablespoons soy sauce
- 1 tablespoon rice vinegar
- 1 tablespoon honey
- 1 tablespoon chopped fresh cilantro (optional)

DIRECTIONS

1. Preheat your Traeger grill to 225°F with the lid closed for about 15 minutes.

2. Pat the chicken legs dry with paper towels to ensure the seasoning adheres well.

3. Rub olive oil over each chicken leg, making sure they are evenly coated.

4. In a small bowl, mix together kosher salt, black pepper, smoked paprika, garlic powder, and onion powder.

5. Season the chicken legs generously with the spice mixture, covering all sides.

6. In a separate bowl, whisk together sweet chili sauce, soy sauce, rice vinegar, and honey to create the glaze.

7. Place the chicken legs directly on the grill grates. Insert the probe into the thickest part of one of the legs, avoiding the bone.

8. Smoke the chicken at 225°F for 1.5 hours.

9. Increase the grill temperature to 375°F and brush the chicken with the sweet chili glaze. Continue to cook for an additional 30 to 45 minutes, basting with glaze every 10 minutes, until the internal temperature reaches 175°F.

10. Once cooked, remove the chicken from the grill and let it rest for 10 minutes before serving. Garnish with chopped fresh cilantro if desired.

Rest time: 10 minutes — Traeger settings: Temperature: 225°F, then 375°F Super Smoke: On Probe Use: Yes — Recommended pellets: Cherry or Apple — Pro tips: For an extra kick, add a teaspoon of sriracha to the glaze. — Suggested sides: Grilled corn on the cob, potato salad, or a fresh garden salad — Nutritional facts (per serving): Calories: 480 Protein: 38g Carbohydrates: 25g Fat: 25g Saturated Fat: 6g Cholesterol: 160mg Sodium: 950mg

32. Grilled Chicken Breasts with Pesto

Cooking Time:

20 to 25 minutes

Preparation Time:

15 minutes

Number of Servings:

4

Difficulty Rating:

Easy

INGREDIENTS

- 4 boneless, skinless chicken breasts
- 1/4 cup olive oil
- 1 teaspoon kosher salt
- 1/2 teaspoon freshly ground black pepper
- 1/2 teaspoon garlic powder
- 1/2 teaspoon onion powder
- 1/2 cup prepared pesto
- 1/4 cup grated Parmesan cheese
- 1 tablespoon lemon juice
- 1 tablespoon chopped fresh basil (optional)

DIRECTIONS

1. Preheat your Traeger grill to 375°F with the lid closed for about 15 minutes.

2. Pat the chicken breasts dry with paper towels to ensure the seasoning adheres well.

3. In a small bowl, mix together olive oil, kosher salt, black pepper, garlic powder, and onion powder.

4. Brush the chicken breasts with the olive oil mixture, ensuring they are evenly coated on all sides.

5. Place the chicken breasts directly on the grill grates. Insert the probe into the thickest part of one of the breasts.

6. Grill the chicken at 375°F for 20 to 25 minutes, or until the internal temperature reaches 165°F.

7. In a small bowl, combine the pesto, Parmesan cheese, and lemon juice.

8. During the last 5 minutes of grilling, brush the pesto mixture over the chicken breasts.

9. Once cooked, remove the chicken from the grill and let it rest for 5 minutes before serving. Garnish with chopped fresh basil if desired.

Rest time: 5 minutes — Traeger settings: Temperature: 375°F Super Smoke: Off Probe Use: Yes — Recommended pellets: Hickory or Apple — Pro tips: For a more intense flavor, marinate the chicken in the olive oil mixture for up to 2 hours before grilling. — Suggested sides: Grilled asparagus, roasted potatoes, or a Caprese salad — Nutritional facts (per serving): Calories: 420 Protein: 50g Carbohydrates: 3g Fat: 24g Saturated Fat: 5g Cholesterol: 130mg Sodium: 750mg

33. Traeger Smoked Chicken Sandwiches

Cooking Time:

1 hour 30 minutes

Preparation Time:

15 minutes

Number of Servings:

4

Difficulty Rating:

Easy

INGREDIENTS

- 4 boneless, skinless chicken thighs
- 1 tablespoon olive oil
- 1 teaspoon kosher salt
- 1/2 teaspoon freshly ground black pepper
- 1 teaspoon smoked paprika
- 1/2 teaspoon garlic powder
- 1/2 teaspoon onion powder
- 1/2 cup barbecue sauce
- 4 brioche buns
- 1 cup coleslaw
- 1/4 cup pickles, sliced

DIRECTIONS

1. Preheat your Traeger grill to 225°F with the lid closed for about 15 minutes.

2. Pat the chicken thighs dry with paper towels to ensure the seasoning adheres well.

3. In a small bowl, mix together olive oil, kosher salt, black pepper, smoked paprika, garlic powder, and onion powder.

4. Rub the seasoning mixture evenly over the chicken thighs, ensuring all sides are coated.

5. Place the chicken thighs directly on the grill grates. Insert the probe into the thickest part of one of the thighs.

6. Smoke the chicken at 225°F for 1 hour.

7. Increase the grill temperature to 375°F and brush the chicken with barbecue sauce. Continue to cook for an additional 20 to 30 minutes, or until the internal temperature reaches 175°F.

8. Once cooked, remove the chicken from the grill and let it rest for 5 minutes.

9. Toast the brioche buns on the grill for 1 to 2 minutes until lightly browned.

10. Assemble the sandwiches by placing a chicken thigh on each bun, topping with coleslaw and pickles.

Rest time: 5 minutes — Traeger settings: Temperature: 225°F, then 375°F Super Smoke: On Probe Use: Yes — Recommended pellets: Hickory or Apple — Pro tips: For added flavor, marinate the chicken in the seasoning mixture for up to 2 hours before grilling. — Suggested sides: Sweet potato fries, grilled corn, or a simple green salad — Nutritional facts (per serving): Calories: 550 Protein: 35g Carbohydrates: 45g Fat: 25g Saturated Fat: 7g Cholesterol: 120mg Sodium: 1050mg

34. Grilled Chicken Fajitas with Peppers

Cooking Time:

25 to 30 minutes

Preparation Time:

20 minutes

Number of Servings:

4

Difficulty Rating:

Easy

INGREDIENTS

- 2 pounds boneless, skinless chicken breasts
- 1/4 cup olive oil
- 1 tablespoon lime juice
- 1 teaspoon kosher salt
- 1/2 teaspoon freshly ground black pepper
- 1 teaspoon chili powder
- 1/2 teaspoon cumin
- 1/2 teaspoon garlic powder
- 1/2 teaspoon onion powder
- 1 red bell pepper, sliced
- 1 yellow bell pepper, sliced
- 1 green bell pepper, sliced
- 1 large onion, sliced
- 8 flour tortillas
- 1/4 cup chopped fresh cilantro (optional)
- Lime wedges for serving

DIRECTIONS

1. Preheat your Traeger grill to 400°F with the lid closed for about 15 minutes.

2. In a large bowl, combine olive oil, lime juice, kosher salt, black pepper, chili powder, cumin, garlic powder, and onion powder.

3. Add the chicken breasts to the bowl, ensuring they are well coated with the marinade. Let them sit for 10 minutes.

4. Place the chicken breasts directly on the grill grates. Insert the probe into the thickest part of one of the breasts.

5. Grill the chicken at 400°F for 15 to 20 minutes, or until the internal temperature reaches 165°F.

6. While the chicken is grilling, toss the sliced bell peppers and onion in any remaining marinade.

7. Once the chicken is cooked, remove it from the grill and let it rest for 5 minutes.

8. Place the peppers and onion directly on the grill grates. Grill for 5 to 7 minutes, or until they are tender and slightly charred.

9. Slice the rested chicken into thin strips.

10. Warm the flour tortillas on the grill for 1 to 2 minutes.

11. Assemble the fajitas by placing chicken strips, grilled peppers, and onions in each tortilla. Garnish with chopped cilantro and serve with lime wedges.

Rest time: 5 minutes — Traeger settings: Temperature: 400°F Super Smoke: Off Probe Use: Yes — Recommended pellets: Mesquite or Pecan — Pro tips: For extra flavor, marinate the chicken for up to 2 hours in the refrigerator. — Suggested sides: Mexican rice, black beans, or a fresh avocado salad — Nutritional facts (per serving): Calories: 480 Protein: 45g Carbohydrates: 40g Fat: 18g Saturated Fat: 3g Cholesterol: 110mg Sodium: 850mg

35. Smoked Chicken Salad with Avocado

Cooking Time:

1 hour 30 minutes

Preparation Time:

20 minutes

Number of Servings:

4

Difficulty Rating:

Easy

INGREDIENTS

- 4 boneless, skinless chicken breasts
- 2 tablespoons olive oil
- 1 teaspoon kosher salt
- 1/2 teaspoon freshly ground black pepper
- 1 teaspoon smoked paprika
- 1/2 teaspoon garlic powder
- 1/2 teaspoon onion powder
- 2 ripe avocados, diced
- 1/2 cup cherry tomatoes, halved
- 1/4 cup red onion, finely chopped
- 1/4 cup fresh cilantro, chopped
- 2 tablespoons lime juice
- 4 cups mixed salad greens

DIRECTIONS

1. Preheat your Traeger grill to 225°F with the lid closed for about 15 minutes.

2. Pat the chicken breasts dry with paper towels to ensure the seasoning adheres well.

3. In a small bowl, mix together olive oil, kosher salt, black pepper, smoked paprika, garlic powder, and onion powder.

4. Rub the seasoning mixture evenly over the chicken breasts, ensuring all sides are coated.

5. Place the chicken breasts directly on the grill grates. Insert the probe into the thickest part of one of the breasts.

6. Smoke the chicken at 225°F for 1 hour.

7. Increase the grill temperature to 375°F and continue to cook for an additional 20 to 30 minutes, or until the internal temperature reaches 165°F.

8. Once cooked, remove the chicken from the grill and let it rest for 5 minutes.

9. While the chicken is resting, in a large bowl, combine diced avocados, cherry tomatoes, red onion, cilantro, and lime juice. Toss gently to mix.

10. Slice the rested chicken into thin strips.

11. Arrange the mixed salad greens on a serving platter. Top with the avocado mixture and sliced chicken.

Rest time: 5 minutes — Traeger settings: Temperature: 225°F, then 375°F Super Smoke: On Probe Use: Yes — Recommended pellets: Apple or Cherry — Pro tips: For added flavor, marinate the chicken in the seasoning mixture for up to 2 hours before grilling. — Suggested sides: Grilled corn on the cob, crusty bread, or a light pasta salad — Nutritional facts (per serving): Calories: 450 Protein: 40g Carbohydrates: 20g Fat: 25g Saturated Fat: 4g Cholesterol: 100mg Sodium: 750mg

36. Traeger Grilled Chicken Pizza

Cooking Time:
35 to 40 minutes

Preparation Time:
20 minutes

Number of Servings:
4

Difficulty Rating:
Medium

INGREDIENTS

- 1 pound boneless, skinless chicken breasts
- 1 tablespoon olive oil
- 1 teaspoon kosher salt
- 1/2 teaspoon freshly ground black pepper
- 1 teaspoon Italian seasoning
- 1/2 teaspoon garlic powder
- 1/2 teaspoon onion powder
- 1 pre-made pizza crust (12-inch)
- 1/2 cup pizza sauce
- 1 1/2 cups shredded mozzarella cheese
- 1/2 cup sliced red onion
- 1/2 cup sliced bell peppers (any color)
- 1/4 cup sliced black olives
- 1/4 cup grated Parmesan cheese
- 1/4 cup fresh basil leaves, torn

DIRECTIONS

1. Preheat your Traeger grill to 375°F with the lid closed for about 15 minutes.

2. In a small bowl, mix together olive oil, kosher salt, black pepper, Italian seasoning, garlic powder, and onion powder.

3. Rub the seasoning mixture evenly over the chicken breasts, ensuring all sides are coated.

4. Place the chicken breasts directly on the grill grates. Insert the probe into the thickest part of one of the breasts.

5. Grill the chicken at 375°F for 20 to 25 minutes, or until the internal temperature reaches 165°F.

6. Once cooked, remove the chicken from the grill and let it rest for 5 minutes.

7. Increase the grill temperature to 450°F.

8. Slice the rested chicken into thin strips.

9. Place the pizza crust on a pizza stone or baking sheet. Spread the pizza sauce evenly over the crust.

10. Sprinkle half of the mozzarella cheese over the sauce.

11. Arrange the sliced chicken, red onion, bell peppers, and black olives evenly over the cheese.

12. Top with the remaining mozzarella cheese and Parmesan cheese.

13. Place the pizza on the grill and cook for 10 to 12 minutes, or until the cheese is melted and bubbly.

14. Remove the pizza from the grill and let it cool for a few minutes.

15. Garnish with fresh basil leaves before slicing and serving.

Rest time: 5 minutes — Traeger settings: Temperature: 375°F, then 450°F Super Smoke: Off Probe Use: Yes — Recommended pellets: Hickory or Oak — Pro tips: For a crispier crust, preheat the pizza stone on the grill for 10 minutes before adding the pizza. — Suggested sides: Caesar salad, garlic bread, or a fresh fruit salad — Nutritional facts (per serving): Calories: 520 Protein: 45g Carbohydrates: 40g Fat: 22g Saturated Fat: 8g Cholesterol: 110mg Sodium: 950mg

TURKEY RECIPES

FOR THE TRAEGER GRILL

37. Traeger Grilled Turkey Tenderloin

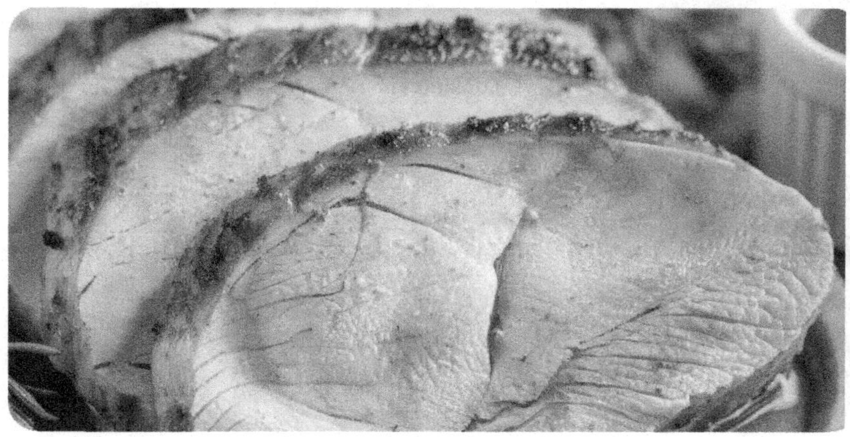

Cooking Time:

25 to 30 minutes

Preparation Time:

10 minutes

Number of Servings:

4

Difficulty Rating:

Easy

INGREDIENTS

- 2 pounds turkey tenderloin
- 3 tablespoons olive oil
- 2 tablespoons lemon juice
- 1 tablespoon Dijon mustard
- 1 tablespoon honey
- 2 teaspoons garlic powder
- 1 teaspoon smoked paprika
- 1 teaspoon kosher salt
- 1/2 teaspoon freshly ground black pepper
- 1/4 teaspoon cayenne pepper (optional)

DIRECTIONS

1. Preheat your Traeger grill to 350°F with the lid closed for about 15 minutes.

2. In a small bowl, whisk together olive oil, lemon juice, Dijon mustard, honey, garlic powder, smoked paprika, kosher salt, black pepper, and cayenne pepper.

3. Place the turkey tenderloins in a large resealable plastic bag or shallow dish. Pour the marinade over the turkey, ensuring it is well coated. Seal the bag or cover the dish and refrigerate for at least 30 minutes, or up to 2 hours for more flavor.

4. Remove the turkey from the marinade and let any excess drip off. Discard the marinade.

5. Place the turkey tenderloins directly on the grill grates. Insert the probe into the thickest part of one of the tenderloins.

6. Grill the turkey at 350°F for 25 to 30 minutes, or until the internal temperature reaches 165°F, turning once halfway through cooking.

7. Once cooked, remove the turkey from the grill and let it rest for 5 minutes before slicing and serving.

Rest time: 5 minutes — Traeger settings: Temperature: 350°F, Super Smoke: Off, Probe Use: Yes — Recommended pellets: Apple or Pecan — Pro tips: For a deeper flavor, marinate the turkey overnight in the refrigerator. — Suggested sides: Grilled asparagus, roasted potatoes, or a fresh garden salad — Nutritional facts (per serving): Calories: 320, Protein: 45g, Carbohydrates: 5g, Fat: 14g, Saturated Fat: 2g, Cholesterol: 110mg, Sodium: 600mg

38. Smoked Turkey Wings with Honey Glaze

Cooking Time:

1.5 to 2 hours

Preparation Time:

15 minutes

Number of Servings:

4

Difficulty Rating:

Medium

INGREDIENTS

- 4 turkey wings
- 2 tablespoons olive oil
- 2 tablespoons kosher salt
- 1 tablespoon smoked paprika
- 1 tablespoon garlic powder
- 1 teaspoon onion powder
- 1 teaspoon ground black pepper
- 1/2 cup honey
- 2 tablespoons apple cider vinegar
- 1 tablespoon soy sauce
- 1 teaspoon crushed red pepper flakes (optional)

DIRECTIONS

1. Preheat your Traeger grill to 225°F with the lid closed for about 15 minutes.

2. Pat the turkey wings dry with paper towels to ensure the seasoning adheres well.

3. In a small bowl, mix together olive oil, kosher salt, smoked paprika, garlic powder, onion powder, and black pepper.

4. Rub the seasoning mixture evenly over the turkey wings, ensuring all sides are coated.

5. Place the turkey wings directly on the grill grates. Insert the probe into the thickest part of one of the wings.

6. Smoke the turkey wings at 225°F for 1.5 to 2 hours, or until the internal temperature reaches 165°F.

7. In a small saucepan, combine honey, apple cider vinegar, soy sauce, and crushed red pepper flakes. Heat over medium-low heat, stirring occasionally, until the glaze is smooth and slightly thickened, about 5 minutes.

8. Once the wings reach 165°F, brush them generously with the honey glaze.

9. Increase the grill temperature to 350°F and continue to cook for an additional 15 to 20 minutes, or until the glaze is caramelized and the internal temperature reaches 175°F.

10. Remove the turkey wings from the grill and let them rest for 10 minutes before serving.

Rest time: 10 minutes — Traeger settings: Temperature: 225°F, then 350°F, Super Smoke: On, Probe Use: Yes — Recommended pellets: Cherry or Apple — Pro tips: For a deeper flavor, marinate the turkey wings in the seasoning mixture overnight in the refrigerator. — Suggested sides: Grilled corn on the cob, potato salad, or coleslaw — Nutritional facts (per serving): Calories: 520, Protein: 45g, Carbohydrates: 30g, Fat: 28g, Saturated Fat: 8g, Cholesterol: 150mg, Sodium: 1100mg

39. Grilled Turkey Skewers with Vegetables

Cooking Time:

15 to 20 minutes

Preparation Time:

15 minutes

Number of Servings:

4

Difficulty Rating:

Easy

INGREDIENTS

- 1.5 pounds turkey breast, cut into 1-inch cubes
- 2 tablespoons olive oil
- 2 tablespoons lemon juice
- 1 tablespoon soy sauce
- 1 tablespoon honey
- 2 teaspoons garlic powder
- 1 teaspoon smoked paprika
- 1 teaspoon kosher salt
- 1/2 teaspoon ground black pepper
- 1 red bell pepper, cut into 1-inch pieces
- 1 yellow bell pepper, cut into 1-inch pieces
- 1 red onion, cut into wedges
- 8 wooden skewers, soaked in water for 30 minutes

DIRECTIONS

1. Preheat your Traeger grill to 375°F with the lid closed for about 15 minutes.

2. In a large bowl, whisk together olive oil, lemon juice, soy sauce, honey, garlic powder, smoked paprika, kosher salt, and black pepper.

3. Add the turkey cubes to the marinade, tossing to coat evenly. Cover and refrigerate for at least 30 minutes, or up to 2 hours for enhanced flavor.

4. Thread the marinated turkey cubes, bell peppers, and onion wedges alternately onto the soaked skewers.

5. Place the skewers directly on the grill grates. Insert the probe into the center of one of the turkey pieces.

6. Grill the skewers at 375°F for 15 to 20 minutes, turning occasionally, until the internal temperature of the turkey reaches 165°F.

7. Once cooked, remove the skewers from the grill and let them rest for 5 minutes before serving.

Rest time: 5 minutes — Traeger settings: Temperature: 375°F, Super Smoke: Off, Probe Use: Yes — Recommended pellets: Hickory or Mesquite — Pro tips: For a more intense flavor, marinate the turkey overnight in the refrigerator. — Suggested sides: Grilled zucchini, couscous salad, or garlic bread — Nutritional facts (per serving): Calories: 350, Protein: 40g, Carbohydrates: 15g, Fat: 15g, Saturated Fat: 2g, Cholesterol: 100mg, Sodium: 750mg

40. Smoked Whole Turkey with Herb Butter

Cooking Time:

3 to 4 hours

Preparation Time:

30 minutes

Number of Servings:

10-12

Difficulty Rating:

Medium

INGREDIENTS

- 1 whole turkey (12-14 pounds)
- 1/2 cup unsalted butter, softened
- 2 tablespoons fresh rosemary, chopped
- 2 tablespoons fresh thyme, chopped
- 2 tablespoons fresh sage, chopped
- 1 tablespoon kosher salt
- 1 tablespoon black pepper
- 1 lemon, halved
- 1 onion, quartered
- 4 cloves garlic, smashed
- 1 cup chicken broth

DIRECTIONS

1. Preheat your Traeger grill to 225°F with the lid closed for about 15 minutes.

2. In a small bowl, combine the softened butter, rosemary, thyme, sage, kosher salt, and black pepper. Mix until well combined.

3. Pat the turkey dry with paper towels. Gently loosen the skin over the breast and thighs, being careful not to tear it.

4. Spread the herb butter mixture evenly under the skin and over the entire surface of the turkey.

5. Stuff the cavity of the turkey with the lemon halves, onion quarters, and smashed garlic cloves.

6. Tie the legs together with kitchen twine and tuck the wing tips under the body.

7. Place the turkey on a roasting rack set inside a large roasting pan. Pour the chicken broth into the bottom of the pan.

8. Insert the probe into the thickest part of the breast, avoiding bone.

9. Smoke the turkey at 225°F for 2.5 to 3 hours, or until the internal temperature reaches 165°F.

10. Once the turkey reaches 165°F, increase the grill temperature to 350°F and continue to cook for an additional 30 to 45 minutes, or until the skin is golden brown and crispy.

11. Remove the turkey from the grill and let it rest for 20 minutes before carving.

Rest time: 20 minutes — Traeger settings: Temperature: 225°F, then 350°F, Super Smoke: On, Probe Use: Yes — Recommended pellets: Hickory or Apple — Pro tips: For extra flavor, prepare the herb butter a day in advance and let it sit in the refrigerator overnight. — Suggested sides: Mashed potatoes, green bean casserole, or cranberry sauce — Nutritional facts (per serving): Calories: 450, Protein: 60g, Carbohydrates: 2g, Fat: 22g, Saturated Fat: 8g, Cholesterol: 200mg, Sodium: 800mg

41. Traeger Grilled Turkey Sausages

Cooking Time:

1.5 to 2 hours

Preparation Time:

45 minutes

Number of Servings:

6

Difficulty Rating:

Medium

INGREDIENTS

- 2 pounds ground turkey
- 1 tablespoon olive oil
- 2 teaspoons garlic powder
- 2 teaspoons onion powder
- 1 teaspoon smoked paprika
- 1 teaspoon dried oregano
- 1 teaspoon kosher salt
- 1/2 teaspoon ground black pepper
- 1/4 teaspoon cayenne pepper (optional, for a bit of heat)
- 1/4 cup cold water
- Natural hog casings, soaked in warm water for 30 minutes

DIRECTIONS

1. In a large bowl, combine ground turkey, olive oil, garlic powder, onion powder, smoked paprika, oregano, kosher salt, black pepper, and cayenne pepper. Mix until well combined.

2. Gradually add cold water to the mixture, stirring until the water is fully incorporated and the mixture is smooth.

3. Rinse the soaked casings under cold water to remove any salt.

4. Attach a sausage stuffer to your stand mixer or use a manual sausage stuffer. Slide the casing onto the stuffer nozzle, leaving a few inches hanging off the end.

5. Carefully fill the casing with the turkey mixture, being cautious not to overstuff. Twist the sausages into 6-inch links.

6. Preheat your Traeger grill to 225°F with the lid closed for about 15 minutes.

7. Place the sausages directly on the grill grates. Insert the probe into the center of one sausage link.

8. Smoke the sausages at 225°F for 1.5 to 2 hours, or until the internal temperature reaches 165°F.

9. Once cooked, remove the sausages from the grill and let them rest for 5 minutes before serving.

Rest time: 5 minutes — Traeger settings: Temperature: 225°F, Super Smoke: On, Probe Use: Yes — Recommended pellets: Hickory or Apple — Pro tips: For a juicier sausage, keep the turkey mixture cold while stuffing. — Suggested sides: Grilled corn on the cob, potato salad, or coleslaw — Nutritional facts (per serving): Calories: 250, Protein: 30g, Carbohydrates: 2g, Fat: 14g, Saturated Fat: 3g, Cholesterol: 85mg, Sodium: 600mg

42. Smoked Turkey Thighs with Maple Glaze

Cooking Time:

2.5 to 3 hours

Preparation Time:

20 minutes

Number of Servings:

4

Difficulty Rating:

Medium

INGREDIENTS

- 4 turkey thighs
- 1/4 cup olive oil
- 1/4 cup maple syrup
- 2 tablespoons apple cider vinegar
- 2 tablespoons Dijon mustard
- 1 tablespoon soy sauce
- 1 tablespoon garlic powder
- 1 tablespoon onion powder
- 1 teaspoon smoked paprika
- 1 teaspoon kosher salt
- 1/2 teaspoon ground black pepper

DIRECTIONS

1. Preheat your Traeger grill to 225°F with the lid closed for about 15 minutes.

2. In a small bowl, whisk together olive oil, maple syrup, apple cider vinegar, Dijon mustard, and soy sauce until well combined.

3. In another bowl, mix garlic powder, onion powder, smoked paprika, kosher salt, and black pepper.

4. Pat the turkey thighs dry with paper towels. Rub the spice mixture evenly over the turkey thighs.

5. Place the turkey thighs directly on the grill grates. Insert the probe into the thickest part of one thigh, avoiding bone.

6. Smoke the turkey thighs at 225°F for 2 to 2.5 hours, or until the internal temperature reaches 165°F.

7. Brush the maple glaze over the turkey thighs every 30 minutes during the smoking process.

8. Once the turkey reaches 165°F, increase the grill temperature to 350°F and continue to cook for an additional 15 to 20 minutes, or until the skin is golden brown and crispy.

9. Remove the turkey thighs from the grill and let them rest for 10 minutes before serving.

Rest time: 10 minutes — Traeger settings: Temperature: 225°F, then 350°F, Super Smoke: On, Probe Use: Yes — Recommended pellets: Maple or Cherry — Pro tips: For a deeper flavor, marinate the turkey thighs in the maple glaze for a few hours before grilling. — Suggested sides: Roasted sweet potatoes, grilled asparagus, or a fresh garden salad — Nutritional facts (per serving): Calories: 480, Protein: 50g, Carbohydrates: 12g, Fat: 25g, Saturated Fat: 6g, Cholesterol: 180mg, Sodium: 750mg

43. Grilled Turkey Cutlets with Lemon Pepper

Cooking Time:
10 to 12 minutes

Preparation Time:
10 minutes

Number of Servings:
4

Difficulty Rating:
Easy

INGREDIENTS

- 4 turkey cutlets (about 1 pound total)
- 2 tablespoons olive oil
- 1 tablespoon lemon juice
- 1 tablespoon lemon zest
- 2 teaspoons lemon pepper seasoning
- 1 teaspoon garlic powder
- 1 teaspoon kosher salt
- 1/2 teaspoon ground black pepper

DIRECTIONS

1. Preheat your Traeger grill to 350°F with the lid closed for about 15 minutes.

2. In a small bowl, combine olive oil, lemon juice, and lemon zest.

3. In another bowl, mix lemon pepper seasoning, garlic powder, kosher salt, and black pepper.

4. Pat the turkey cutlets dry with paper towels. Brush both sides of the cutlets with the olive oil mixture.

5. Sprinkle the seasoning mixture evenly over both sides of the cutlets.

6. Place the turkey cutlets directly on the grill grates.

7. Grill the cutlets at 350°F for 10 to 12 minutes, flipping halfway through, until the internal temperature reaches 165°F.

8. Remove the cutlets from the grill and let them rest for 5 minutes before serving.

Rest time: 5 minutes — Traeger settings: Temperature: 350°F, Super Smoke: Off, Probe Use: No — Recommended pellets: Lemon or Alder — Pro tips: For extra flavor, marinate the cutlets in the olive oil mixture for 30 minutes before grilling. — Suggested sides: Grilled vegetables, quinoa salad, or lemon herb rice — Nutritional facts (per serving): Calories: 220, Protein: 30g, Carbohydrates: 2g, Fat: 10g, Saturated Fat: 2g, Cholesterol: 75mg, Sodium: 500mg

LAMB RECIPES

FOR THE TRAEGER GRILL

44. Smoked Lamb Shoulder with BBQ Glaze

Cooking Time:

4 to 5 hours

Preparation Time:

30 minutes

Number of Servings:

6 to 8

Difficulty Rating:

Medium

INGREDIENTS

- 4 pounds lamb shoulder, bone-in
- 1/4 cup olive oil
- 1/4 cup apple cider vinegar
- 1/4 cup brown sugar
- 1/4 cup ketchup
- 2 tablespoons Worcestershire sauce
- 2 tablespoons Dijon mustard
- 1 tablespoon smoked paprika
- 1 tablespoon garlic powder
- 1 tablespoon onion powder
- 1 tablespoon kosher salt
- 1 teaspoon ground black pepper
- 1 teaspoon cayenne pepper
- 1/2 cup BBQ sauce

DIRECTIONS

1. Preheat your Traeger grill to 225°F with the lid closed for about 15 minutes.

2. In a small bowl, mix together olive oil, apple cider vinegar, brown sugar, ketchup, Worcestershire sauce, Dijon mustard, smoked paprika, garlic powder, onion powder, kosher salt, black pepper, and cayenne pepper to create a marinade.

3. Pat the lamb shoulder dry with paper towels. Rub the marinade all over the lamb, ensuring it is evenly coated.

4. Insert the probe into the thickest part of the lamb, avoiding bone.

5. Place the lamb directly on the grill grates.

6. Smoke the lamb at 225°F for 4 to 5 hours, or until the internal temperature reaches 195°F for tender, pull-apart meat.

7. During the last 30 minutes of cooking, brush the lamb with BBQ sauce every 10 minutes.

8. Remove the lamb from the grill and let it rest for 20 minutes before slicing or shredding.

Rest time: 20 minutes — Traeger settings: Temperature: 225°F, Super Smoke: On, Probe Use: Yes — Recommended pellets: Mesquite or Oak — Pro tips: For a more intense flavor, marinate the lamb overnight in the refrigerator. — Suggested sides: Coleslaw, cornbread, or grilled corn on the cob — Nutritional facts (per serving): Calories: 520, Protein: 45g, Carbohydrates: 15g, Fat: 32g, Saturated Fat: 12g, Cholesterol: 140mg, Sodium: 850mg

45. Grilled Lamb Burgers with Feta and Spinach

Cooking Time:

10 to 12 minutes

Preparation Time:

15 minutes

Number of Servings:

4

Difficulty Rating:

Easy

INGREDIENTS

- 2 pounds ground lamb
- 1 cup crumbled feta cheese
- 1 cup fresh spinach, chopped
- 1/4 cup red onion, finely chopped
- 2 cloves garlic, minced
- 1 tablespoon fresh mint, chopped
- 1 tablespoon fresh parsley, chopped
- 1 teaspoon ground cumin
- 1 teaspoon kosher salt
- 1/2 teaspoon ground black pepper
- 1/4 teaspoon cayenne pepper
- 4 hamburger buns
- 1/4 cup tzatziki sauce

DIRECTIONS

1. In a large bowl, combine ground lamb, feta cheese, spinach, red onion, garlic, mint, parsley, cumin, kosher salt, black pepper, and cayenne pepper. Mix gently until all ingredients are evenly incorporated.

2. Divide the mixture into 4 equal portions and shape each into a patty about 1/2 inch thick.

3. Preheat your Traeger grill to 400°F with the lid closed for about 15 minutes.

4. Place the lamb patties directly on the grill grates. Grill at 400°F for 5 to 6 minutes per side, or until the internal temperature reaches 160°F.

5. During the last 2 minutes of grilling, place the hamburger buns on the grill to toast lightly.

6. Remove the lamb burgers and buns from the grill. Let the burgers rest for 5 minutes.

7. Assemble the burgers by placing each patty on a bun and topping with a dollop of tzatziki sauce.

Rest time: 5 minutes — Traeger settings: Temperature: 400°F, Super Smoke: Off, Probe Use: No — Recommended pellets: Hickory or Apple — Pro tips: For added flavor, let the patties rest in the refrigerator for 30 minutes before grilling. — Suggested sides: Greek salad, sweet potato fries, or grilled asparagus — Nutritional facts (per serving): Calories: 520, Protein: 38g, Carbohydrates: 28g, Fat: 32g, Saturated Fat: 12g, Cholesterol: 110mg, Sodium: 850mg

46. Traeger Smoked Lamb Ribs with Honey Glaze

Cooking Time:

3 to 4 hours

Preparation Time:

20 minutes

Number of Servings:

4 to 6

Difficulty Rating:

Medium

INGREDIENTS

- 3 pounds lamb ribs
- 1/4 cup olive oil
- 1/4 cup honey
- 2 tablespoons apple cider vinegar
- 2 tablespoons soy sauce
- 1 tablespoon Dijon mustard
- 1 tablespoon smoked paprika
- 1 tablespoon garlic powder
- 1 tablespoon onion powder
- 1 teaspoon kosher salt
- 1 teaspoon ground black pepper
- 1/2 teaspoon cayenne pepper

DIRECTIONS

1. Preheat your Traeger grill to 225°F with the lid closed for about 15 minutes.

2. In a small bowl, mix together olive oil, honey, apple cider vinegar, soy sauce, Dijon mustard, smoked paprika, garlic powder, onion powder, kosher salt, black pepper, and cayenne pepper to create a glaze.

3. Pat the lamb ribs dry with paper towels. Rub the glaze all over the ribs, ensuring they are evenly coated.

4. Insert the probe into the thickest part of the ribs, avoiding bone.

5. Place the lamb ribs directly on the grill grates.

6. Smoke the ribs at 225°F for 3 to 4 hours, or until the internal temperature reaches 190°F for tender meat.

7. During the last 30 minutes of cooking, brush the ribs with additional glaze every 10 minutes.

8. Remove the ribs from the grill and let them rest for 15 minutes before slicing.

Rest time: 15 minutes — Traeger settings: Temperature: 225°F, Super Smoke: On, Probe Use: Yes — Recommended pellets: Cherry or Pecan — Pro tips: For a deeper flavor, marinate the ribs in the glaze overnight in the refrigerator. — Suggested sides: Roasted potatoes, grilled vegetables, or a fresh garden salad — Nutritional facts (per serving): Calories: 480, Protein: 35g, Carbohydrates: 18g, Fat: 30g, Saturated Fat: 12g, Cholesterol: 120mg, Sodium: 780mg

47. Grilled Lamb Loin with Lemon and Thyme

Cooking Time:

20 to 25 minutes

Preparation Time:

15 minutes

Number of Servings:

4

Difficulty Rating:

Medium

INGREDIENTS

- 2 pounds lamb loin, trimmed
- 1/4 cup olive oil
- 2 tablespoons fresh lemon juice
- 1 tablespoon lemon zest
- 2 tablespoons fresh thyme leaves, chopped
- 4 cloves garlic, minced
- 1 teaspoon kosher salt
- 1/2 teaspoon ground black pepper

DIRECTIONS

1. In a small bowl, whisk together olive oil, lemon juice, lemon zest, thyme, garlic, kosher salt, and black pepper to create a marinade.

2. Place the lamb loin in a resealable plastic bag or shallow dish. Pour the marinade over the lamb, ensuring it is well coated. Seal the bag or cover the dish and refrigerate for at least 2 hours, or overnight for best results.

3. Preheat your Traeger grill to 375°F with the lid closed for about 15 minutes.

4. Remove the lamb loin from the marinade and let it sit at room temperature for 15 minutes. Discard the marinade.

5. Insert the probe into the thickest part of the lamb loin.

6. Place the lamb loin directly on the grill grates. Grill at 375°F for 20 to 25 minutes, or until the internal temperature reaches 145°F for medium-rare.

7. Remove the lamb from the grill and let it rest for 10 minutes before slicing.

Rest time: 10 minutes — Traeger settings: Temperature: 375°F, Super Smoke: Off, Probe Use: Yes — Recommended pellets: Oak or Mesquite — Pro tips: For a more intense flavor, marinate the lamb loin overnight in the refrigerator. — Suggested sides: Grilled zucchini, couscous salad, or roasted garlic potatoes — Nutritional facts (per serving): Calories: 450, Protein: 38g, Carbohydrates: 2g, Fat: 32g, Saturated Fat: 12g, Cholesterol: 110mg, Sodium: 480mg

48. Smoked Lamb Shanks with Red Wine Sauce

Cooking Time:

3 to 4 hours

Preparation Time:

20 minutes

Number of Servings:

4

Difficulty Rating:

Medium

INGREDIENTS

- 4 lamb shanks
- 2 tablespoons olive oil
- 1 large onion, chopped
- 4 cloves garlic, minced
- 2 cups red wine
- 2 cups beef broth
- 2 tablespoons tomato paste
- 2 sprigs fresh rosemary
- 2 sprigs fresh thyme
- 1 teaspoon kosher salt
- 1 teaspoon ground black pepper

DIRECTIONS

1. Preheat your Traeger grill to 250°F with the lid closed for about 15 minutes.

2. Pat the lamb shanks dry with paper towels. Season them with kosher salt and black pepper.

3. In a large cast-iron skillet, heat olive oil over medium-high heat. Sear the lamb shanks on all sides until browned, about 8 minutes. Remove the shanks and set aside.

4. In the same skillet, add chopped onion and minced garlic. Sauté until the onion is translucent, about 5 minutes.

5. Stir in the tomato paste and cook for 1 minute. Add red wine, beef broth, rosemary, and thyme. Bring to a simmer.

6. Return the lamb shanks to the skillet, ensuring they are submerged in the liquid.

7. Insert the probe into the thickest part of one of the shanks, avoiding bone.

8. Place the skillet on the grill grates. Smoke the lamb shanks at 250°F for 3 to 4 hours, or until the internal temperature reaches 195°F for tender meat.

9. Remove the skillet from the grill and let the shanks rest in the sauce for 15 minutes before serving.

Rest time: 15 minutes — Traeger settings: Temperature: 250°F, Super Smoke: On, Probe Use: Yes — Recommended pellets: Hickory or Oak — Pro tips: For a richer sauce, reduce the liquid on the stovetop after removing the shanks. — Suggested sides: Mashed potatoes, steamed green beans, or crusty bread — Nutritional facts (per serving): Calories: 620, Protein: 50g, Carbohydrates: 10g, Fat: 40g, Saturated Fat: 15g, Cholesterol: 160mg, Sodium: 850mg

49. Traeger Grilled Lamb Skewers with Tzatziki

Cooking Time:

10 to 12 minutes

Preparation Time:

20 minutes

Number of Servings:

4

Difficulty Rating:

Medium

INGREDIENTS

- 2 pounds lamb shoulder, cut into 1-inch cubes
- 1/4 cup olive oil
- 3 tablespoons fresh lemon juice
- 2 tablespoons fresh oregano, chopped
- 4 cloves garlic, minced
- 1 teaspoon kosher salt
- 1/2 teaspoon ground black pepper
- 1 large cucumber, peeled, seeded, and grated
- 1 cup plain Greek yogurt
- 1 tablespoon fresh dill, chopped
- 1 tablespoon fresh mint, chopped
- 1 tablespoon red wine vinegar
- 1/2 teaspoon kosher salt
- 1/4 teaspoon ground black pepper
- 8 wooden skewers, soaked in water for 30 minutes

DIRECTIONS

1. In a large bowl, combine olive oil, lemon juice, oregano, garlic, kosher salt, and black pepper. Add lamb cubes and toss to coat. Cover and refrigerate for at least 2 hours, or overnight for best results.

2. Preheat your Traeger grill to 400°F with the lid closed for about 15 minutes.

3. Thread marinated lamb cubes onto soaked skewers, leaving a little space between each piece.

4. Place skewers directly on the grill grates. Grill at 400°F for 10 to 12 minutes, turning occasionally, until the internal temperature reaches 145°F for medium-rare.

5. While the lamb is grilling, prepare the tzatziki sauce. In a medium bowl, combine grated cucumber, Greek yogurt, dill, mint, red wine vinegar, kosher salt, and black pepper. Mix well and refrigerate until ready to serve.

6. Remove lamb skewers from the grill and let them rest for 5 minutes before serving with tzatziki sauce.

Rest time: 5 minutes — Traeger settings: Temperature: 400°F, Super Smoke: Off, Probe Use: Yes — Recommended pellets: Apple or Cherry — Pro tips: For extra flavor, marinate the lamb overnight and serve with warm pita bread. — Suggested sides: Greek salad, roasted potatoes, or grilled vegetables — Nutritional facts (per serving): Calories: 520, Protein: 45g, Carbohydrates: 8g, Fat: 34g, Saturated Fat: 12g, Cholesterol: 130mg, Sodium: 720mg

50. Smoked Rack of Lamb with Dijon Crust

Cooking Time:

1.5 to 2 hours

Preparation Time:

20 minutes

Number of Servings:

4

Difficulty Rating:

Medium

INGREDIENTS

- 2 racks of lamb, frenched (about 1.5 pounds each)
- 1/4 cup Dijon mustard
- 2 tablespoons olive oil
- 4 cloves garlic, minced
- 1 tablespoon fresh rosemary, chopped
- 1 tablespoon fresh thyme, chopped
- 1 teaspoon kosher salt
- 1/2 teaspoon ground black pepper
- 1 cup panko breadcrumbs
- 1/4 cup grated Parmesan cheese

DIRECTIONS

1. Preheat your Traeger grill to 225°F with the lid closed for about 15 minutes.

2. In a small bowl, mix together Dijon mustard, olive oil, minced garlic, rosemary, thyme, kosher salt, and black pepper.

3. Pat the racks of lamb dry with paper towels. Brush the mustard mixture evenly over the lamb racks.

4. In a separate bowl, combine panko breadcrumbs and Parmesan cheese. Press the breadcrumb mixture onto the mustard-coated lamb racks, ensuring an even crust.

5. Insert the probe into the thickest part of one of the racks, avoiding bone.

6. Place the lamb racks directly on the grill grates, bone side down. Smoke at 225°F for 1.5 to 2 hours, or until the internal temperature reaches 130°F for medium-rare.

7. Increase the grill temperature to 400°F and continue to cook for an additional 5 to 10 minutes to crisp the crust.

8. Remove the lamb racks from the grill and let them rest for 10 minutes before slicing and serving.

Rest time: 10 minutes — Traeger settings: Temperature: 225°F, then 400°F, Super Smoke: On, Probe Use: Yes — Recommended pellets: Cherry or Apple — Pro tips: For a more intense flavor, marinate the lamb in the mustard mixture overnight in the refrigerator. — Suggested sides: Roasted asparagus, garlic mashed potatoes, or a fresh garden salad — Nutritional facts (per serving): Calories: 680, Protein: 55g, Carbohydrates: 15g, Fat: 45g, Saturated Fat: 18g, Cholesterol: 160mg, Sodium: 850mg

WILD GAME RECIPES

FOR THE TRAEGER GRILL

51. Traeger Grilled Duck Breast with Orange Glaze

Cooking Time:

12 to 16 minutes

Preparation Time:

15 minutes

Number of Servings:

4

Difficulty Rating:

Medium

INGREDIENTS

- 4 duck breasts (about 6 ounces each)
- 1 tablespoon olive oil
- 1 teaspoon kosher salt
- 1/2 teaspoon ground black pepper
- 1/2 cup orange marmalade
- 2 tablespoons soy sauce
- 1 tablespoon rice vinegar
- 1 tablespoon honey
- 1 teaspoon grated fresh ginger
- 1/2 teaspoon garlic powder

DIRECTIONS

1. Preheat your Traeger grill to 375°F with the lid closed for about 15 minutes.

2. Pat the duck breasts dry with paper towels. Score the skin in a crosshatch pattern, being careful not to cut into the meat.

3. Rub the duck breasts with olive oil, kosher salt, and ground black pepper.

4. In a small saucepan over medium heat, combine orange marmalade, soy sauce, rice vinegar, honey, grated ginger, and garlic powder. Stir until well combined and heated through, about 5 minutes. Remove from heat and set aside.

5. Place the duck breasts skin side down directly on the grill grates. Grill at 375°F for 6 to 8 minutes, or until the skin is crispy and golden brown.

6. Flip the duck breasts and brush with the orange glaze. Continue grilling for another 6 to 8 minutes, or until the internal temperature reaches 135°F for medium-rare.

7. Remove the duck breasts from the grill and let them rest for 5 minutes before slicing and serving.

Rest time: 5 minutes — Traeger settings: Temperature: 375°F, Super Smoke: Off, Probe Use: Yes — Recommended pellets: Apple or Cherry — Pro tips: For extra flavor, marinate the duck breasts in the glaze mixture for 2 hours before grilling. — Suggested sides: Wild rice pilaf, grilled asparagus, or a citrus salad — Nutritional facts (per serving): Calories: 450, Protein: 35g, Carbohydrates: 20g, Fat: 25g, Saturated Fat: 7g, Cholesterol: 120mg, Sodium: 780mg

52. Smoked Pheasant with Herb Butter

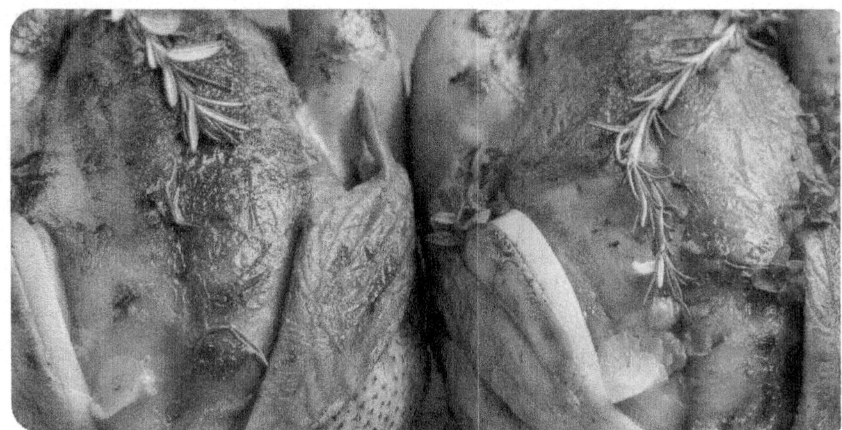

Cooking Time:

2 to 3 hours

Preparation Time:

20 minutes

Number of Servings:

4 to 6

Difficulty Rating:

Medium

INGREDIENTS

- 2 whole pheasants, cleaned and patted dry
- 1/2 cup unsalted butter, softened
- 2 tablespoons fresh rosemary, finely chopped
- 2 tablespoons fresh thyme, finely chopped
- 2 tablespoons fresh parsley, finely chopped
- 1 tablespoon lemon zest
- 1 tablespoon kosher salt
- 1 teaspoon ground black pepper
- 1 lemon, quartered
- 1 head of garlic, halved crosswise

DIRECTIONS

1. Preheat your Traeger grill to 225°F with the lid closed for about 15 minutes.

2. In a small bowl, combine softened butter, rosemary, thyme, parsley, lemon zest, kosher salt, and black pepper. Mix until well combined to create the herb butter.

3. Gently loosen the skin of each pheasant by sliding your fingers between the skin and the breast meat. Be careful not to tear the skin.

4. Spread half of the herb butter under the skin of each pheasant, ensuring even coverage.

5. Stuff the cavity of each pheasant with two lemon quarters and half of the garlic head.

6. Tie the legs of each pheasant together with kitchen twine to ensure even cooking.

7. Insert the probe into the thickest part of one of the pheasant breasts, avoiding bone.

8. Place the pheasants directly on the grill grates, breast side up. Smoke at 225°F for 2 to 3 hours, or until the internal temperature reaches 165°F.

9. Remove the pheasants from the grill and let them rest for 10 minutes before carving and serving.

Rest time: 10 minutes — Traeger settings: Temperature: 225°F, Super Smoke: On, Probe Use: Yes — Recommended pellets: Apple or Cherry — Pro tips: For an extra burst of flavor, marinate the pheasants in a mixture of olive oil, lemon juice, and herbs for 2 hours before applying the herb butter. — Suggested sides: Roasted root vegetables, garlic mashed potatoes, or a fresh green salad — Nutritional facts (per serving): Calories: 520, Protein: 45g, Carbohydrates: 5g, Fat: 35g, Saturated Fat: 15g, Cholesterol: 180mg, Sodium: 780mg

53. Grilled Elk Burgers with Cheddar

Cooking Time:

12 to 14 minutes

Preparation Time:

15 minutes

Number of Servings:

4

Difficulty Rating:

Easy

INGREDIENTS

- 2 pounds ground elk
- 1 teaspoon kosher salt
- 1/2 teaspoon ground black pepper
- 1 teaspoon garlic powder
- 1 teaspoon onion powder
- 1 tablespoon Worcestershire sauce
- 4 slices sharp cheddar cheese
- 4 brioche burger buns
- 1 tablespoon olive oil
- Lettuce, tomato slices, and red onion rings for serving

DIRECTIONS

1. Preheat your Traeger grill to 400°F with the lid closed for about 15 minutes.

2. In a large bowl, combine ground elk, kosher salt, black pepper, garlic powder, onion powder, and Worcestershire sauce. Mix gently until just combined.

3. Divide the mixture into 4 equal portions and shape each into a patty about 3/4 inch thick.

4. Brush each patty lightly with olive oil to prevent sticking.

5. Place the patties directly on the grill grates. Grill at 400°F for 5 to 6 minutes per side, or until the internal temperature reaches 160°F.

6. During the last minute of cooking, place a slice of cheddar cheese on each patty and close the lid to melt the cheese.

7. Remove the patties from the grill and let them rest for 5 minutes.

8. Toast the brioche buns on the grill for 1 to 2 minutes, until golden brown.

9. Assemble the burgers with lettuce, tomato slices, and red onion rings.

Rest time: 5 minutes — Traeger settings: Temperature: 400°F, Super Smoke: Off, Probe Use: Yes — Recommended pellets: Hickory or Mesquite — Pro tips: For added flavor, mix in a tablespoon of your favorite barbecue sauce into the elk mixture before forming the patties. — Suggested sides: Sweet potato fries, coleslaw, or grilled corn on the cob — Nutritional facts (per serving): Calories: 550, Protein: 45g, Carbohydrates: 30g, Fat: 30g, Saturated Fat: 12g, Cholesterol: 120mg, Sodium: 850mg

54. Smoked Rabbit with Garlic and Thyme

Cooking Time:

2 to 3 hours

Preparation Time:

20 minutes

Number of Servings:

4 to 6

Difficulty Rating:

Medium

INGREDIENTS

- 2 whole rabbits, cleaned and patted dry
- 1/4 cup olive oil
- 6 cloves garlic, minced
- 2 tablespoons fresh thyme leaves, chopped
- 1 tablespoon kosher salt
- 1 teaspoon ground black pepper
- 1 lemon, sliced
- 1/4 cup white wine

DIRECTIONS

1. Preheat your Traeger grill to 225°F with the lid closed for about 15 minutes.

2. In a small bowl, combine olive oil, minced garlic, chopped thyme, kosher salt, and black pepper. Mix well to create a marinade.

3. Rub the marinade all over the rabbits, ensuring even coverage.

4. Stuff the cavity of each rabbit with lemon slices.

5. Place the rabbits in a shallow dish and pour white wine over them. Cover and refrigerate for at least 1 hour, or overnight for more flavor.

6. Remove the rabbits from the refrigerator and let them come to room temperature for about 30 minutes before grilling.

7. Insert the probe into the thickest part of one of the rabbit thighs, avoiding bone.

8. Place the rabbits directly on the grill grates. Smoke at 225°F for 2 to 3 hours, or until the internal temperature reaches 160°F.

9. Remove the rabbits from the grill and let them rest for 10 minutes before carving and serving.

Rest time: 10 minutes — Traeger settings: Temperature: 225°F, Super Smoke: On, Probe Use: Yes — Recommended pellets: Apple or Cherry — Pro tips: For a deeper flavor, marinate the rabbits overnight. — Suggested sides: Grilled asparagus, wild rice pilaf, or a mixed greens salad — Nutritional facts (per serving): Calories: 480, Protein: 50g, Carbohydrates: 4g, Fat: 28g, Saturated Fat: 6g, Cholesterol: 150mg, Sodium: 720mg

55. Traeger Grilled Quail with Honey Mustard

Cooking Time:

20 to 25 minutes

Preparation Time:

15 minutes

Number of Servings:

4

Difficulty Rating:

Medium

INGREDIENTS

- 8 whole quail, cleaned and patted dry
- 1/4 cup olive oil
- 1/4 cup honey
- 1/4 cup Dijon mustard
- 2 tablespoons apple cider vinegar
- 1 tablespoon soy sauce
- 1 teaspoon garlic powder
- 1 teaspoon onion powder
- 1 teaspoon kosher salt
- 1/2 teaspoon ground black pepper

DIRECTIONS

1. Preheat your Traeger grill to 375°F with the lid closed for about 15 minutes.

2. In a medium bowl, whisk together olive oil, honey, Dijon mustard, apple cider vinegar, soy sauce, garlic powder, onion powder, kosher salt, and black pepper to create a marinade.

3. Place the quail in a large resealable plastic bag and pour the marinade over them. Seal the bag and massage gently to ensure the quail are evenly coated.

4. Refrigerate the quail in the marinade for at least 1 hour, or up to 4 hours for more flavor.

5. Remove the quail from the refrigerator and let them come to room temperature for about 30 minutes before grilling.

6. Insert the probe into the thickest part of one of the quail breasts, avoiding bone.

7. Place the quail directly on the grill grates. Grill at 375°F for 20 to 25 minutes, or until the internal temperature reaches 160°F, turning once halfway through cooking.

8. Remove the quail from the grill and let them rest for 5 minutes before serving.

Rest time: 5 minutes — Traeger settings: Temperature: 375°F, Super Smoke: Off, Probe Use: Yes — Recommended pellets: Pecan or Apple — Pro tips: For a more intense flavor, marinate the quail overnight. — Suggested sides: Grilled vegetables, roasted potatoes, or a fresh garden salad — Nutritional facts (per serving): Calories: 450, Protein: 38g, Carbohydrates: 20g, Fat: 24g, Saturated Fat: 5g, Cholesterol: 120mg, Sodium: 780mg

56. Smoked Goose with Apple Cider Glaze

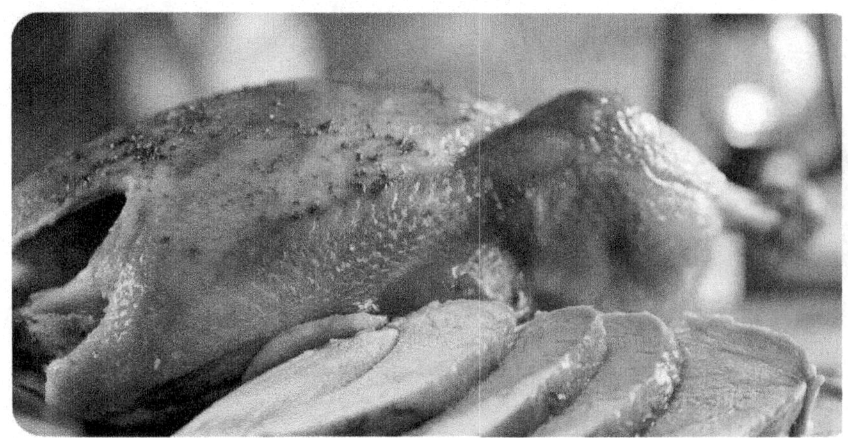

Cooking Time:

3 to 4 hours

Preparation Time:

30 minutes

Number of Servings:

8 to 10

Difficulty Rating:

Medium

INGREDIENTS

- 1 whole goose, about 10-12 pounds, cleaned and patted dry
- 1/4 cup olive oil
- 1 tablespoon kosher salt
- 1 teaspoon ground black pepper
- 1 teaspoon garlic powder
- 1 teaspoon onion powder
- 1 cup apple cider
- 1/4 cup apple cider vinegar
- 1/4 cup brown sugar
- 2 tablespoons Dijon mustard
- 1 tablespoon soy sauce
- 1 teaspoon ground cinnamon
- 1/2 teaspoon ground cloves

DIRECTIONS

1. Preheat your Traeger grill to 225°F with the lid closed for about 15 minutes.

2. In a small bowl, mix together olive oil, kosher salt, black pepper, garlic powder, and onion powder. Rub this mixture all over the goose, ensuring even coverage.

3. In a saucepan over medium heat, combine apple cider, apple cider vinegar, brown sugar, Dijon mustard, soy sauce, cinnamon, and cloves. Stir until the sugar dissolves and the mixture thickens slightly, about 5 minutes. Remove from heat and set aside.

4. Insert the probe into the thickest part of the goose breast, avoiding bone.

5. Place the goose directly on the grill grates. Smoke at 225°F for 3 to 4 hours, or until the internal temperature reaches 160°F.

6. During the last hour of cooking, baste the goose with the apple cider glaze every 20 minutes.

7. Once the goose reaches the desired temperature, remove it from the grill and let it rest for 20 minutes before carving and serving.

Rest time: 20 minutes — Traeger settings: Temperature: 225°F, Super Smoke: On, Probe Use: Yes — Recommended pellets: Apple or Cherry — Pro tips: For a more intense flavor, marinate the goose overnight in the apple cider glaze. — Suggested sides: Roasted root vegetables, mashed potatoes, or a cranberry walnut salad — Nutritional facts (per serving): Calories: 650, Protein: 60g, Carbohydrates: 18g, Fat: 38g, Saturated Fat: 10g, Cholesterol: 220mg, Sodium: 820mg

57. Grilled Bison Ribeye with Chimichurri

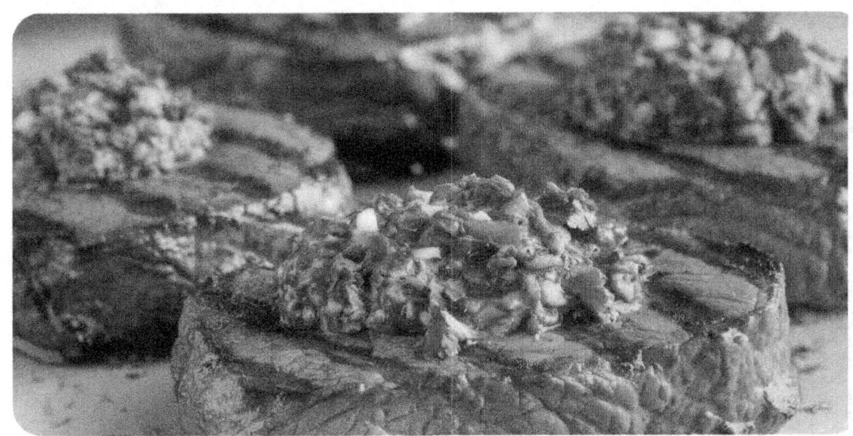

Cooking Time:

8 to 10 minutes

Preparation Time:

15 minutes

Number of Servings:

4

Difficulty Rating:

Easy

INGREDIENTS

- 4 bison ribeye steaks, about 1 inch thick
- 1/4 cup olive oil
- 2 teaspoons kosher salt
- 1 teaspoon ground black pepper
- 1 teaspoon garlic powder
- 1 teaspoon onion powder
- 1 cup fresh parsley, finely chopped
- 1/4 cup fresh cilantro, finely chopped
- 4 cloves garlic, minced
- 1/2 cup olive oil
- 1/4 cup red wine vinegar
- 1 teaspoon crushed red pepper flakes
- 1/2 teaspoon kosher salt
- 1/4 teaspoon ground black pepper

DIRECTIONS

1. Preheat your Traeger grill to 450°F with the lid closed for about 15 minutes.

2. In a small bowl, mix together olive oil, kosher salt, black pepper, garlic powder, and onion powder. Rub this mixture evenly over both sides of the bison ribeye steaks.

3. For the chimichurri sauce, combine parsley, cilantro, garlic, olive oil, red wine vinegar, crushed red pepper flakes, kosher salt, and black pepper in a medium bowl. Stir well to combine and set aside.

4. Insert the probe into the thickest part of one of the bison ribeye steaks.

5. Place the steaks directly on the grill grates. Grill at 450°F for 4 to 5 minutes per side, or until the internal temperature reaches 130°F for medium-rare.

6. Remove the steaks from the grill and let them rest for 5 minutes before serving.

7. Serve the bison ribeye steaks with a generous spoonful of chimichurri sauce on top.

Rest time: 5 minutes — Traeger settings: Temperature: 450°F, Super Smoke: Off, Probe Use: Yes — Recommended pellets: Hickory or Mesquite — Pro tips: For a more intense flavor, marinate the bison ribeye steaks in the olive oil mixture for up to 2 hours before grilling. — Suggested sides: Grilled asparagus, roasted sweet potatoes, or a mixed greens salad — Nutritional facts (per serving): Calories: 520, Protein: 48g, Carbohydrates: 4g, Fat: 36g, Saturated Fat: 10g, Cholesterol: 120mg, Sodium: 780mg

58. Smoked Antelope Tenderloin with Red Wine Sauce

Cooking Time:

1.5 to 2 hours

Number of Servings:

4

Preparation Time:

20 minutes

Difficulty Rating:

Medium

INGREDIENTS

- 2 pounds antelope tenderloin, trimmed
- 2 tablespoons olive oil
- 1 tablespoon kosher salt
- 1 teaspoon ground black pepper
- 1 teaspoon garlic powder
- 1 teaspoon onion powder
- 1 cup red wine
- 1/2 cup beef broth
- 2 tablespoons unsalted butter
- 2 cloves garlic, minced
- 1 tablespoon fresh rosemary, chopped
- 1 tablespoon fresh thyme, chopped

DIRECTIONS

1. Preheat your Traeger grill to 225°F with the lid closed for about 15 minutes.

2. In a small bowl, mix together olive oil, kosher salt, black pepper, garlic powder, and onion powder. Rub this mixture evenly over the antelope tenderloin.

3. Insert the probe into the thickest part of the tenderloin.

4. Place the tenderloin directly on the grill grates. Smoke at 225°F for 1.5 to 2 hours, or until the internal temperature reaches 130°F for medium-rare.

5. While the tenderloin is smoking, prepare the red wine sauce. In a saucepan over medium heat, combine red wine, beef broth, and minced garlic. Bring to a simmer and reduce by half, about 10 minutes.

6. Remove the saucepan from heat and whisk in the butter, rosemary, and thyme until the sauce is smooth and slightly thickened.

7. Once the tenderloin reaches the desired temperature, remove it from the grill and let it rest for 10 minutes before slicing.

8. Serve the sliced antelope tenderloin with the red wine sauce drizzled on top.

Rest time: 10 minutes — Traeger settings: Temperature: 225°F, Super Smoke: On, Probe Use: Yes — Recommended pellets: Oak or Pecan — Pro tips: For a deeper flavor, marinate the antelope tenderloin in the olive oil mixture for up to 4 hours before smoking. — Suggested sides: Grilled asparagus, garlic mashed potatoes, or a fresh arugula salad — Nutritional facts (per serving): Calories: 420, Protein: 48g, Carbohydrates: 4g, Fat: 22g, Saturated Fat: 8g, Cholesterol: 140mg, Sodium: 780mg

FISH AND SEAFOOD RECIPES
FOR THE TRAEGER GRILL

59. Smoked Lobster Tails with Garlic Butter

Cooking Time:

45 to 60 minutes

Preparation Time:

15 minutes

Number of Servings:

4

Difficulty Rating:

Medium

INGREDIENTS

- 4 lobster tails (about 6 ounces each)
- 1/2 cup unsalted butter, melted
- 4 cloves garlic, minced
- 1 tablespoon fresh lemon juice
- 1 teaspoon smoked paprika
- 1/2 teaspoon kosher salt
- 1/4 teaspoon ground black pepper
- Fresh parsley, chopped, for garnish
- Lemon wedges, for serving

DIRECTIONS

1. Preheat your Traeger grill to 225°F with the lid closed for about 15 minutes.

2. Using kitchen shears, carefully cut the top shell of each lobster tail down the center, stopping at the base of the tail. Gently pull the shell apart to expose the meat.

3. In a small bowl, combine the melted butter, minced garlic, lemon juice, smoked paprika, kosher salt, and black pepper. Mix well.

4. Brush the garlic butter mixture generously over the exposed lobster meat.

5. Insert the probe into the thickest part of one of the lobster tails.

6. Place the lobster tails directly on the grill grates, meat side up. Smoke at 225°F for 45 to 60 minutes, or until the internal temperature reaches 140°F.

7. Remove the lobster tails from the grill and let them rest for 5 minutes.

8. Garnish with fresh parsley and serve with lemon wedges.

Rest time: 5 minutes — Traeger settings: Temperature: 225°F, Super Smoke: On, Probe Use: Yes — Recommended pellets: Cherry or Apple — Pro tips: For a richer flavor, prepare the garlic butter a day in advance and let it sit in the refrigerator overnight. — Suggested sides: Grilled asparagus, garlic bread, or a Caesar salad — Nutritional facts (per serving): Calories: 320, Protein: 28g, Carbohydrates: 2g, Fat: 22g, Saturated Fat: 12g, Cholesterol: 180mg, Sodium: 480mg

60. Grilled Mahi Mahi with Mango Salsa

Cooking Time:

10 to 12 minutes

Preparation Time:

15 minutes

Number of Servings:

4

Difficulty Rating:

Easy

INGREDIENTS

- 4 mahi mahi fillets (about 6 ounces each)
- 2 tablespoons olive oil
- 1 teaspoon kosher salt
- 1/2 teaspoon ground black pepper
- 1 teaspoon smoked paprika
- 1 lime, cut into wedges
- 1 ripe mango, peeled, pitted, and diced
- 1/4 cup red onion, finely chopped
- 1/4 cup red bell pepper, diced
- 1 jalapeño, seeded and minced
- 2 tablespoons fresh cilantro, chopped
- 1 tablespoon lime juice
- 1/4 teaspoon kosher salt

DIRECTIONS

1. Preheat your Traeger grill to 375°F with the lid closed for about 15 minutes.

2. In a small bowl, combine olive oil, kosher salt, black pepper, and smoked paprika. Mix well.

3. Brush the mahi mahi fillets with the olive oil mixture on both sides.

4. Place the fillets directly on the grill grates. Grill at 375°F for 10 to 12 minutes, turning once halfway through, until the fish is opaque and flakes easily with a fork.

5. While the fish is grilling, prepare the mango salsa by combining the diced mango, red onion, red bell pepper, jalapeño, cilantro, lime juice, and kosher salt in a medium bowl. Mix gently.

6. Remove the mahi mahi from the grill and let it rest for 3 minutes.

7. Serve the grilled mahi mahi topped with mango salsa and lime wedges on the side.

Rest time: 3 minutes — Traeger settings: Temperature: 375°F, Super Smoke: Off, Probe Use: No — Recommended pellets: Alder or Apple — Pro tips: For a spicier kick, leave the seeds in the jalapeño when preparing the salsa. — Suggested sides: Coconut rice, grilled corn on the cob, or a mixed greens salad — Nutritional facts (per serving): Calories: 280, Protein: 30g, Carbohydrates: 15g, Fat: 10g, Saturated Fat: 2g, Cholesterol: 90mg, Sodium: 480mg

61. Smoked Scallops with Bacon

Cooking Time:

45 to 60 minutes

Preparation Time:

15 minutes

Number of Servings:

4

Difficulty Rating:

Medium

INGREDIENTS

- 1 pound large sea scallops
- 8 slices bacon, cut in half
- 1 tablespoon olive oil
- 1 teaspoon kosher salt
- 1/2 teaspoon ground black pepper
- 1 tablespoon fresh lemon juice
- 2 tablespoons fresh parsley, chopped

DIRECTIONS

1. Preheat your Traeger grill to 225°F with the lid closed for about 15 minutes.

2. Rinse the scallops under cold water and pat them dry with paper towels.

3. Wrap each scallop with a half slice of bacon and secure with a toothpick.

4. In a small bowl, combine olive oil, kosher salt, black pepper, and lemon juice. Mix well.

5. Brush the scallops with the olive oil mixture on all sides.

6. Insert the probe into the center of one of the scallops.

7. Place the scallops directly on the grill grates. Smoke at 225°F for 45 to 60 minutes, or until the internal temperature reaches 145°F and the bacon is crispy.

8. Remove the scallops from the grill and let them rest for 5 minutes.

9. Garnish with fresh parsley before serving.

Rest time: 5 minutes — Traeger settings: Temperature: 225°F, Super Smoke: On, Probe Use: Yes — Recommended pellets: Hickory or Apple — Pro tips: For extra flavor, marinate the scallops in the olive oil mixture for 30 minutes before wrapping them in bacon. — Suggested sides: Grilled vegetables, garlic mashed potatoes, or a fresh garden salad — Nutritional facts (per serving): Calories: 320, Protein: 25g, Carbohydrates: 3g, Fat: 22g, Saturated Fat: 7g, Cholesterol: 70mg, Sodium: 680mg

62. Traeger Grilled Tuna Steaks with Soy Glaze

Cooking Time:

6 to 8 minutes

Preparation Time:

15 minutes

Number of Servings:

4

Difficulty Rating:

Medium

INGREDIENTS

- 4 tuna steaks (about 6 ounces each)
- 1/4 cup soy sauce
- 2 tablespoons honey
- 1 tablespoon rice vinegar
- 1 tablespoon sesame oil
- 1 teaspoon fresh ginger, grated
- 2 cloves garlic, minced
- 1/4 teaspoon red pepper flakes
- 1 tablespoon sesame seeds
- 2 green onions, thinly sliced

DIRECTIONS

1. Preheat your Traeger grill to 400°F with the lid closed for about 15 minutes.

2. In a small bowl, whisk together soy sauce, honey, rice vinegar, sesame oil, ginger, garlic, and red pepper flakes.

3. Place the tuna steaks in a shallow dish and pour half of the soy glaze over them, reserving the other half for later. Let the tuna marinate for 10 minutes, turning once.

4. Remove the tuna from the marinade and pat dry with paper towels. Discard the used marinade.

5. Place the tuna steaks directly on the grill grates. Grill at 400°F for 3 to 4 minutes per side, or until the tuna is seared on the outside and slightly pink in the center.

6. Remove the tuna from the grill and let it rest for 5 minutes.

7. Drizzle the reserved soy glaze over the tuna steaks.

8. Garnish with sesame seeds and sliced green onions before serving.

Rest time: 5 minutes — Traeger settings: Temperature: 400°F, Super Smoke: Off, Probe Use: No — Recommended pellets: Mesquite or Cherry — Pro tips: For a deeper flavor, marinate the tuna steaks for up to 30 minutes in the refrigerator. — Suggested sides: Grilled asparagus, jasmine rice, or a cucumber salad — Nutritional facts (per serving): Calories: 320, Protein: 40g, Carbohydrates: 10g, Fat: 12g, Saturated Fat: 2g, Cholesterol: 60mg, Sodium: 780mg

63. Smoked Catfish with Cajun Spice

Cooking Time:

1 to 1.5 hours

Preparation Time:

10 minutes

Number of Servings:

4

Difficulty Rating:

Easy

INGREDIENTS

- 4 catfish fillets (about 6 ounces each)
- 2 tablespoons olive oil
- 2 tablespoons Cajun seasoning
- 1 teaspoon garlic powder
- 1 teaspoon onion powder
- 1/2 teaspoon smoked paprika
- 1/2 teaspoon cayenne pepper (optional, for extra heat)
- 1 lemon, cut into wedges

DIRECTIONS

1. Preheat your Traeger grill to 225°F with the lid closed for about 15 minutes.

2. Rinse the catfish fillets under cold water and pat them dry with paper towels.

3. In a small bowl, mix together olive oil, Cajun seasoning, garlic powder, onion powder, smoked paprika, and cayenne pepper.

4. Brush the catfish fillets with the spice mixture on both sides, ensuring an even coating.

5. Insert the probe into the thickest part of one of the fillets.

6. Place the catfish fillets directly on the grill grates. Smoke at 225°F for 1 to 1.5 hours, or until the internal temperature reaches 145°F and the fish flakes easily with a fork.

7. Remove the catfish from the grill and let them rest for 5 minutes.

8. Serve with lemon wedges for squeezing over the top.

Rest time: 5 minutes — Traeger settings: Temperature: 225°F, Super Smoke: On, Probe Use: Yes — Recommended pellets: Pecan or Alder — Pro tips: For a milder flavor, reduce the amount of cayenne pepper or omit it entirely. — Suggested sides: Coleslaw, cornbread, or grilled corn on the cob — Nutritional facts (per serving): Calories: 280, Protein: 30g, Carbohydrates: 2g, Fat: 16g, Saturated Fat: 3g, Cholesterol: 80mg, Sodium: 480mg

64. Grilled Swordfish with Chimichurri

Cooking Time:

10 to 12 minutes

Preparation Time:

15 minutes

Number of Servings:

4

Difficulty Rating:

Medium

INGREDIENTS

- 4 swordfish steaks (about 8 ounces each)
- 1/4 cup olive oil
- 2 tablespoons fresh lemon juice
- 1 teaspoon salt
- 1/2 teaspoon black pepper
- 1 cup fresh parsley, finely chopped
- 1/4 cup fresh cilantro, finely chopped
- 1/4 cup fresh oregano, finely chopped
- 3 cloves garlic, minced
- 1/2 teaspoon red pepper flakes
- 1/4 cup red wine vinegar

DIRECTIONS

1. Preheat your Traeger grill to 375°F with the lid closed for about 15 minutes.

2. In a small bowl, whisk together olive oil, lemon juice, salt, and black pepper.

3. Brush the swordfish steaks with the olive oil mixture on both sides, ensuring an even coating.

4. In a separate bowl, combine parsley, cilantro, oregano, garlic, red pepper flakes, and red wine vinegar to make the chimichurri sauce. Mix well and set aside.

5. Place the swordfish steaks directly on the grill grates. Grill at 375°F for 5 to 6 minutes per side, or until the internal temperature reaches 145°F and the fish flakes easily with a fork.

6. Remove the swordfish from the grill and let them rest for 5 minutes.

7. Spoon the chimichurri sauce generously over the grilled swordfish before serving.

Rest time: 5 minutes — Traeger settings: Temperature: 375°F, Super Smoke: Off, Probe Use: No — Recommended pellets: Hickory or Apple — Pro tips: For a more intense flavor, prepare the chimichurri sauce a few hours in advance and let it sit in the refrigerator to allow the flavors to meld. — Suggested sides: Grilled vegetables, quinoa salad, or roasted potatoes — Nutritional facts (per serving): Calories: 420, Protein: 45g, Carbohydrates: 5g, Fat: 25g, Saturated Fat: 4g, Cholesterol: 90mg, Sodium: 600mg

VEGETABLE RECIPES

FOR THE TRAEGER GRILL

65. Grilled Zucchini with Parmesan and Basil

Cooking Time:

8 to 10 minutes

Preparation Time:

10 minutes

Number of Servings:

4

Difficulty Rating:

Easy

INGREDIENTS

- 4 medium zucchinis, sliced lengthwise into 1/4-inch thick strips
- 3 tablespoons olive oil
- 1 teaspoon salt
- 1/2 teaspoon black pepper
- 1/2 cup grated Parmesan cheese
- 1/4 cup fresh basil leaves, chopped
- 1 tablespoon lemon juice

DIRECTIONS

1. Preheat your Traeger grill to 400°F with the lid closed for about 15 minutes.

2. In a large bowl, toss the zucchini slices with olive oil, salt, and black pepper until evenly coated.

3. Place the zucchini slices directly on the grill grates.

4. Grill at 400°F for 8 to 10 minutes, turning once, until the zucchini is tender and has grill marks.

5. Remove the zucchini from the grill and transfer to a serving platter.

6. Sprinkle grated Parmesan cheese and chopped basil over the grilled zucchini.

7. Drizzle with lemon juice before serving.

Rest time: None — Traeger settings: Temperature: 400°F, Super Smoke: Off, Probe Use: No — Recommended pellets: Hickory or Oak — Pro tips: For added flavor, try adding a pinch of red pepper flakes to the zucchini before grilling. — Suggested sides: Grilled chicken, pasta salad, or a fresh green salad — Nutritional facts (per serving): Calories: 120, Protein: 5g, Carbohydrates: 8g, Fat: 9g, Saturated Fat: 2g, Cholesterol: 5mg, Sodium: 450mg

66. Smoked Bell Peppers with Olive Oil and Sea Salt

Cooking Time:

60 to 75 minutes

Preparation Time:

10 minutes

Number of Servings:

4

Difficulty Rating:

Easy

INGREDIENTS

- 4 large bell peppers (red, yellow, or orange)
- 2 tablespoons olive oil
- 1 teaspoon sea salt
- 1/2 teaspoon black pepper

DIRECTIONS

1. Preheat your Traeger grill to 225°F with the lid closed for about 15 minutes.

2. Wash and dry the bell peppers. Cut them in half lengthwise and remove the seeds and membranes.

3. In a small bowl, mix olive oil, sea salt, and black pepper.

4. Brush the inside and outside of each bell pepper half with the olive oil mixture.

5. Place the bell pepper halves directly on the grill grates, cut side up.

6. Smoke at 225°F for 60 to 75 minutes, until the peppers are tender and have a nice smoky aroma.

7. Remove the peppers from the grill and let them rest for 5 minutes before serving.

Rest time: 5 minutes — Traeger settings: Temperature: 225°F, Super Smoke: On, Probe Use: No — Recommended pellets: Apple or Maple — Pro tips: For a touch of sweetness, drizzle a little balsamic glaze over the smoked peppers before serving. — Suggested sides: Grilled corn on the cob, quinoa salad, or a light pasta dish — Nutritional facts (per serving): Calories: 80, Protein: 1g, Carbohydrates: 7g, Fat: 6g, Saturated Fat: 1g, Cholesterol: 0mg, Sodium: 300mg

67. Traeger Grilled Corn on the Cob with Chili Lime Butter

Cooking Time:

20 to 25 minutes

Preparation Time:

10 minutes

Number of Servings:

4

Difficulty Rating:

Easy

INGREDIENTS

- 4 ears of corn, husked
- 1/4 cup unsalted butter, softened
- 1 teaspoon chili powder
- 1 lime, zested and juiced
- 1/2 teaspoon salt
- 1/4 teaspoon black pepper
- 1/4 cup chopped fresh cilantro

DIRECTIONS

1. Preheat your Traeger grill to 375°F with the lid closed for about 15 minutes.

2. In a small bowl, combine the softened butter, chili powder, lime zest, lime juice, salt, and black pepper. Mix until well combined.

3. Brush each ear of corn with the chili lime butter, ensuring an even coating.

4. Place the corn directly on the grill grates.

5. Grill at 375°F for 20 to 25 minutes, turning every 5 minutes, until the corn is tender and has a slight char.

6. Remove the corn from the grill and let it rest for 5 minutes.

7. Sprinkle with chopped cilantro before serving.

Rest time: 5 minutes — Traeger settings: Temperature: 375°F, Super Smoke: Off, Probe Use: No — Recommended pellets: Mesquite or Cherry — Pro tips: For an extra kick, add a pinch of cayenne pepper to the chili lime butter. — Suggested sides: Grilled steak, potato salad, or coleslaw — Nutritional facts (per serving): Calories: 180, Protein: 3g, Carbohydrates: 22g, Fat: 10g, Saturated Fat: 6g, Cholesterol: 25mg, Sodium: 250mg

68. Smoked Cauliflower Steaks with Curry Rub

Cooking Time:

20 to 25 minutes

Preparation Time:

10 minutes

Number of Servings:

3 to 4

Difficulty Rating:

Easy

INGREDIENTS

- 1 large head of cauliflower
- 2 tablespoons olive oil
- 1 tablespoon curry powder
- 1 teaspoon garlic powder
- 1 teaspoon onion powder
- 1 teaspoon sea salt
- 1/2 teaspoon black pepper

DIRECTIONS

1. Preheat your Traeger grill to 350°F with the lid closed for about 15 minutes.

2. Remove the leaves and trim the stem of the cauliflower, keeping the core intact.

3. Slice the cauliflower into 1-inch thick steaks. You should get about 3 to 4 steaks from one head.

4. In a small bowl, mix olive oil, curry powder, garlic powder, onion powder, sea salt, and black pepper.

5. Brush both sides of each cauliflower steak with the curry rub mixture, ensuring an even coating.

6. Place the cauliflower steaks directly on the grill grates.

7. Grill at 350°F for 20 to 25 minutes, flipping halfway through, until the cauliflower is tender and has a nice char.

8. Remove the cauliflower steaks from the grill and let them rest for 5 minutes before serving.

Rest time: 5 minutes — Traeger settings: Temperature: 350°F, Super Smoke: Off, Probe Use: No — Recommended pellets: Hickory or Pecan — Pro tips: For an extra layer of flavor, sprinkle a little smoked paprika over the cauliflower steaks before serving. — Suggested sides: Grilled asparagus, wild rice, or a fresh green salad — Nutritional facts (per serving): Calories: 120, Protein: 3g, Carbohydrates: 10g, Fat: 8g, Saturated Fat: 1g, Cholesterol: 0mg, Sodium: 400mg

69. Grilled Brussels Sprouts with Bacon and Maple Syrup

Cooking Time:

30 to 35 minutes

Preparation Time:

10 minutes

Number of Servings:

4

Difficulty Rating:

Easy

INGREDIENTS

- 1 pound Brussels sprouts, trimmed and halved
- 4 slices thick-cut bacon, chopped
- 2 tablespoons olive oil
- 1 tablespoon maple syrup
- 1 teaspoon sea salt
- 1/2 teaspoon black pepper

DIRECTIONS

1. Preheat your Traeger grill to 400°F with the lid closed for about 15 minutes.

2. In a large bowl, toss the halved Brussels sprouts with olive oil, sea salt, and black pepper until evenly coated.

3. Spread the Brussels sprouts in a single layer on a grill-safe baking sheet or cast-iron skillet.

4. Sprinkle the chopped bacon evenly over the Brussels sprouts.

5. Place the baking sheet or skillet directly on the grill grates.

6. Grill at 400°F for 25 to 30 minutes, stirring halfway through, until the Brussels sprouts are tender and the bacon is crispy.

7. Drizzle the maple syrup over the Brussels sprouts and bacon, then toss to combine.

8. Grill for an additional 5 minutes to allow the maple syrup to caramelize slightly.

9. Remove from the grill and let rest for 5 minutes before serving.

Rest time: 5 minutes — Traeger settings: Temperature: 400°F, Super Smoke: Off, Probe Use: No — Recommended pellets: Apple or Maple — Pro tips: For added flavor, sprinkle a pinch of red pepper flakes over the Brussels sprouts before grilling. — Suggested sides: Grilled chicken, mashed potatoes, or a fresh garden salad — Nutritional facts (per serving): Calories: 220, Protein: 7g, Carbohydrates: 18g, Fat: 15g, Saturated Fat: 4g, Cholesterol: 20mg, Sodium: 600mg

70. Smoked Sweet Potatoes with Cinnamon and Honey

Cooking Time:

45 to 60 minutes

Preparation Time:

10 minutes

Number of Servings:

4

Difficulty Rating:

Easy

INGREDIENTS

- 4 medium sweet potatoes
- 2 tablespoons olive oil
- 1 teaspoon sea salt
- 1 teaspoon ground cinnamon
- 2 tablespoons honey

DIRECTIONS

1. Preheat your Traeger grill to 375°F with the lid closed for about 15 minutes.

2. Wash and scrub the sweet potatoes thoroughly, then pat them dry with a paper towel.

3. Pierce each sweet potato several times with a fork to allow steam to escape during cooking.

4. Rub each sweet potato with olive oil, ensuring an even coating.

5. Sprinkle sea salt evenly over the sweet potatoes.

6. Place the sweet potatoes directly on the grill grates.

7. Grill at 375°F for 45 to 60 minutes, or until the sweet potatoes are tender and can be easily pierced with a fork.

8. Remove the sweet potatoes from the grill and let them rest for 5 minutes.

9. Slice each sweet potato open lengthwise and sprinkle with ground cinnamon.

10. Drizzle honey over the top of each sweet potato before serving.

Rest time: 5 minutes — Traeger settings: Temperature: 375°F, Super Smoke: Off, Probe Use: No — Recommended pellets: Cherry or Apple — Pro tips: For a touch of heat, add a pinch of cayenne pepper along with the cinnamon. — Suggested sides: Grilled chicken, roasted vegetables, or a fresh green salad — Nutritional facts (per serving): Calories: 180, Protein: 2g, Carbohydrates: 40g, Fat: 4g, Saturated Fat: 1g, Cholesterol: 0mg, Sodium: 300mg

TRAEGER GRILL DESSERT RECIPES

71. Smoked Chocolate Lava Cake

Cooking Time:

12 to 14 minutes

Preparation Time:

15 minutes

Number of Servings:

4

Difficulty Rating:

Medium

INGREDIENTS

- 1 cup semisweet chocolate chips
- 1/2 cup unsalted butter, plus extra for greasing
- 1 cup powdered sugar
- 2 large eggs
- 2 large egg yolks
- 1 teaspoon vanilla extract
- 1/2 cup all-purpose flour
- 1/4 teaspoon salt
- Nonstick cooking spray

DIRECTIONS

1. Preheat your Traeger grill to 425°F with the lid closed for about 15 minutes.

2. In a microwave-safe bowl, combine the chocolate chips and 1/2 cup of unsalted butter. Microwave in 30-second intervals, stirring in between, until the mixture is smooth and fully melted.

3. Stir in the powdered sugar until well combined.

4. Add the eggs and egg yolks, one at a time, mixing well after each addition.

5. Stir in the vanilla extract.

6. Gently fold in the flour and salt until just combined, being careful not to overmix.

7. Grease four 6-ounce ramekins with butter and lightly dust with flour, tapping out any excess.

8. Divide the batter evenly among the prepared ramekins.

9. Place the ramekins directly on the grill grates.

10. Grill at 425°F for 12 to 14 minutes, or until the edges are firm but the center is still soft.

11. Carefully remove the ramekins from the grill and let them rest for 1 minute.

12. Run a knife around the edges of each cake to loosen, then invert onto individual plates.

Rest time: 1 minute — Traeger settings: Temperature: 425°F, Super Smoke: Off, Probe Use: No — Recommended pellets: Hickory or Mesquite — Pro tips: For an extra indulgent touch, add a piece of dark chocolate in the center of each ramekin before grilling. — Suggested sides: Fresh berries or a scoop of vanilla ice cream — Nutritional facts (per serving): Calories: 450, Protein: 6g, Carbohydrates: 50g, Fat: 28g, Saturated Fat: 16g, Cholesterol: 180mg, Sodium: 150mg

72. Traeger Grilled Pineapple Upside-Down Cake

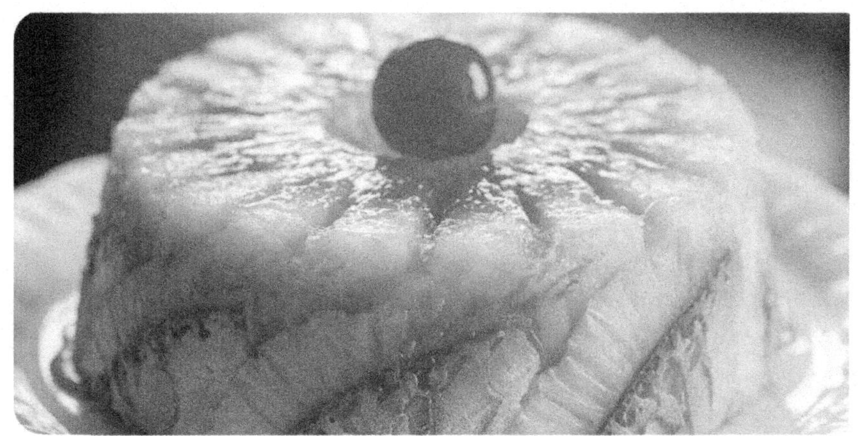

Cooking Time:

35 to 40 minutes

Preparation Time:

20 minutes

Number of Servings:

8

Difficulty Rating:

Medium

INGREDIENTS

- 1/2 cup unsalted butter, melted
- 1 cup packed brown sugar
- 1 can (20 oz) pineapple slices, drained
- 10 maraschino cherries
- 1 1/2 cups all-purpose flour
- 1 cup granulated sugar
- 1 1/2 teaspoons baking powder
- 1/2 teaspoon salt
- 1/2 cup whole milk
- 1/3 cup vegetable oil
- 1 teaspoon vanilla extract
- 2 large eggs

DIRECTIONS

1. Preheat your Traeger grill to 350°F with the lid closed for about 15 minutes.

2. Pour the melted butter into a 12-inch cast iron skillet, ensuring it coats the bottom evenly.

3. Sprinkle the brown sugar over the melted butter in the skillet.

4. Arrange the pineapple slices over the brown sugar, placing a maraschino cherry in the center of each pineapple ring.

5. In a large mixing bowl, combine the flour, granulated sugar, baking powder, and salt.

6. In a separate bowl, whisk together the milk, vegetable oil, vanilla extract, and eggs until well combined.

7. Gradually add the wet ingredients to the dry ingredients, stirring until just combined. Be careful not to overmix.

8. Pour the batter evenly over the pineapple and cherries in the skillet.

9. Place the skillet directly on the grill grates.

10. Grill at 350°F for 35 to 40 minutes, or until a toothpick inserted into the center of the cake comes out clean.

11. Carefully remove the skillet from the grill and let it rest for 10 minutes.

12. Run a knife around the edges of the cake to loosen, then invert onto a serving platter.

Rest time: 10 minutes — Traeger settings: Temperature: 350°F, Super Smoke: Off, Probe Use: No — Recommended pellets: Apple or Cherry — Pro tips: For a tropical twist, add a splash of coconut rum to the batter before grilling. — Suggested sides: Vanilla ice cream or whipped cream — Nutritional facts (per serving): Calories: 420, Protein: 4g, Carbohydrates: 65g, Fat: 18g, Saturated Fat: 9g, Cholesterol: 75mg, Sodium: 220mg

73. Smoked Apple Crisp

Cooking Time:

45 to 50 minutes

Preparation Time:

20 minutes

Number of Servings:

8

Difficulty Rating:

Easy

INGREDIENTS

- 6 large Granny Smith apples, peeled, cored, and sliced
- 1 tablespoon lemon juice
- 1/2 cup granulated sugar
- 1/2 cup packed brown sugar
- 1 teaspoon ground cinnamon
- 1/4 teaspoon ground nutmeg
- 1/4 teaspoon salt
- 1 cup all-purpose flour
- 1 cup old-fashioned oats
- 1/2 cup unsalted butter, melted

DIRECTIONS

1. Preheat your Traeger grill to 350°F with the lid closed for about 15 minutes.

2. In a large bowl, toss the apple slices with lemon juice to prevent browning.

3. Add the granulated sugar, 1/4 cup of the brown sugar, cinnamon, nutmeg, and salt to the apples. Mix until the apples are evenly coated.

4. Transfer the apple mixture to a 9x13-inch baking dish, spreading it out evenly.

5. In a separate bowl, combine the flour, oats, and remaining 1/4 cup of brown sugar.

6. Pour the melted butter over the flour mixture and stir until crumbly.

7. Sprinkle the oat mixture evenly over the apples in the baking dish.

8. Place the baking dish directly on the grill grates.

9. Grill at 350°F for 45 to 50 minutes, or until the topping is golden brown and the apples are tender.

10. Carefully remove the baking dish from the grill and let it rest for 10 minutes before serving.

Rest time: 10 minutes — Traeger settings: Temperature: 350°F, Super Smoke: Off, Probe Use: No — Recommended pellets: Apple or Pecan — Pro tips: For an extra burst of flavor, add a handful of chopped pecans or walnuts to the topping mixture before grilling. — Suggested sides: Vanilla ice cream or whipped cream — Nutritional facts (per serving): Calories: 350, Protein: 3g, Carbohydrates: 60g, Fat: 14g, Saturated Fat: 8g, Cholesterol: 30mg, Sodium: 100mg

Kitchen Measurement Conversion Tables

Liquid or Volume Measures (approximate)			
1 teaspoon		1/3 tablespoon	5 ml
1 tablespoon	1/2 fluid ounce	3 teaspoons	15 ml 15 cc
2 tablespoons	1 fluid ounce	1/8 cup, 6 teaspoons	30 ml, 30 cc
1/4 cup	2 fluid ounces	4 tablespoons	59 ml
1/3 cup	2 2/3 fluid ounces	5 tablespoons & 1 teaspoon	79 ml
1/2 cup	4 fluid ounces	8 tablespoons	118 ml
2/3 cup	5 1/3 fluid ounces	10 tablespoons & 2 teaspoons	158 ml
3/4 cup	6 fluid ounces	12 tablespoons	177 ml
7/8 cup	7 fluid ounces	14 tablespoons	207 ml
1 cup	8 fluid ounces/ 1/2 pint	16 tablespoons	237 ml
2 cups	16 fluid ounces/ 1 pint	32 tablespoons	473 ml
4 cups	32 fluid ounces	1 quart	946 ml
1 pint	16 fluid ounces/ 1 pint	32 tablespoons	473 ml
2 pints	32 fluid ounces	1 quart	946 ml 0.946 liters
8 pints	1 gallon/ 128 fluid ounces	4 quarts	3785 ml 3.78 liters
4 quarts	1 gallon/128 fluid ounces	1 gallon	3785 ml 3.78 liters
1 liter	1.057 quarts		1000 ml
1 gallon	4 quarts	128 fluid ounces	3785 ml 3.78 liters
Dry Or Weight Measurements (approximate)			
1 ounce			30 grams (28.35 g)
2 ounces			55 grams
3 ounces			85 grams
4 ounces	1/4 pound		125 grams
8 ounces	1/2 pound		240 grams
12 ounces	3/4 pound		375 grams
16 ounces	1 pound		454 grams
32 ounces	2 pounds		907 grams
1/4 pound	4 ounces		125 grams
1/2 pound	8 ounces		240 grams
3/4 pound	12 ounces		375 grams
1 pound	16 ounces		454 grams
2 pounds	32 ounces		907 grams
1 kilogram	2.2 pounds/ 35.2 ounces		1000 gram

INDEX

Made in the USA
Coppell, TX
06 April 2026